START TODAY!

W. S.

START TODAY!

Praise for
RUN IT
LIKE YOU'LL SELL IT

Wayne's methodology of identifying business risks and maximizing a sustainable cash flow for the business develops for the seller (and the buyer, as well) a better picture of what the business will look like in the future and the potential risk and reward levers that will significantly impact the ultimate value of the business (especially in those industries that are selling at double-digit multiples of EBITDA).—**Eric Parnes, Retired CPA Partner, PricewaterhouseCoopers**

With Run It Like You'll Sell It, *Wayne Slavitt has created the definitive roadmap for business owners to prepare their businesses for sale. His approach is a sound one: you are always preparing your business for sale. As a result, this book is appropriate for owners of all businesses at all times, whether it is long before an anticipated sale, or one that is already involved in the sale process. Wayne outlines best practices, [and] tells some success stories, along with some horror stories. All of it is very informative, sometimes humorous, and very educational.*

This book is very complete, unpacking the full range of topics from valuing a business, the sales process, legal and financial matters and many more, all in an easy-to-understand format without the use of buzzwords. To those who own a business now without an inclination to sell it soon, my suggestion is to read this book and keep it on your shelf. Refer to it from time to time, and for your business, Run It Like You'll Sell It!—**Peter J. Nelson, Sun Oak Capital**

Run It Like You'll Sell It is a concise, well-written and highly informative book for anyone considering selling their business, now or in the future. With decades of advisory experience to draw from, Wayne cogently breaks down the sale process into its component parts, from start to finish, and in doing so makes what represents a daunting prospect for many business owners much more comfortable and understandable in the end.

Although this slender volume contains many useful insights, I especially liked the analogy of preparing for the sale of a business to the preparatory groundwork one must undertake for the sale of a home - an experience all of us can relate to.

The book is designed to provide the business owner with the necessary information to maximize the value derived from a sale. Since for most owners this is a once-in-a- lifetime experience, the importance of "getting it right" cannot be overstated.

A business owner will be well-rewarded by diligent implementation of the lessons and information this book imparts.—**John E. Romundstad, Attorney at Law**

I have many clients who own their own companies. Until now, we had no resource like *Run It Like You'll Sell It* to guide business owners through the landmines they will face when selling their companies. This is a complicated process, especially if you want to do it right. Wayne is able to break down the concept of business value into just two variables, making it so much easier for business owners to maximize the value of their companies and realize much higher returns. I wish we had this book years ago.—**Don Trojan, CPA**

RUN IT LIKE YOU'LL SELL IT

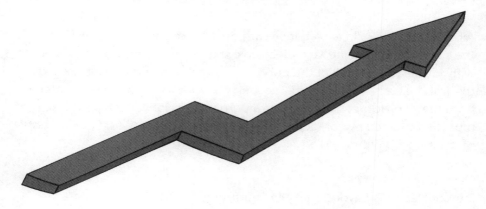

Adopting the Seller's Mindset to
Maximize the Value of Your Business

WAYNE SLAVITT

Copyright © 2021 by Wayne Slavitt

All rights reserved. In accordance with the US Copyright Act of 1976, the scanning, uploading, and electronic sharing of any part of this book without the permission of the publisher constitutes unlawful piracy and theft of the author's intellectual property. If you would like to use material from the book (other than for review purposes), prior written permission must be obtained by contacting the publisher. Thank you for your support of the author's rights.

Text: Wayne Slavitt
Interior Design & Layout: Danielle Smith-Boldt

Hardcover ISBN: 978-1-68515-504-9
Ebook ISBN: 978-1-68515-505-6

TABLE OF CONTENTS

Introduction 9

THE PRELIMINARIES

Chapter 1   The Seller's Mindset 15

Chapter 2   The Need to Be Ready 21

Chapter 3   A Primer on Business Value 29

Chapter 4   The Value Quarterback 33

THE PLANNING PHASE

Chapter 5	Assessing Risk	43
Chapter 6	Growing EBITDA	47
Chapter 7	A Case Study on Turbocharging Business Value	53
Chapter 8	Telling Your Story	57
Chapter 9	Financial Data	61
Chapter 10	Taxes	69
Chapter 11	Customers	73
Chapter 12	Vendors	77
Chapter 13	Capital Expenditures	79
Chapter 14	Debt	83
Chapter 15	Ownership	85
Chapter 16	Gap Analysis	89
Chapter 17	Legal	93
Chapter 18	Employees	97
Chapter 19	Real Estate	101
Chapter 20	Finding Your Buyer	103
Chapter 21	Trusted Advisors	107
Chapter 22	Sell-Side Quality of Earnings Report	111

THE SELLING PHASE

Chapter 23   Negotiating Your Sale............................115

Chapter 24   Due Diligence 119

Chapter 25   The Definitive Agreements 123

Chapter 26   Working Capital................................127

Chapter 27   Negative Issues During Due Diligence..............131

Conclusions *135*

About Wayne Slavitt and The PrimeMark Group™ *137*

INTRODUCTION

If you aren't already aware of what I am about to tell you, then reading this book may be one of the best things you've done in a very long time. Whether you are a business owner or know someone who is, the odds of succeeding in selling a company is only about one in five. That's right: 80% of the companies that attempt to sell their businesses actually fail at doing so. As few as 20% of companies that are put on the market ever sell. Performance like that won't even get you a swing of the bat in the minor leagues.

Why do you think so many business owners fail to sell their companies? Why is it so difficult to be successful at one of the most important events of your life?

Perhaps the most common reason why business owners are unsuccessful in selling their companies is that they fail to properly prepare far enough in advance for an eventual sale. They simply wait too long before they start thinking about selling, consumed instead with the burdens of growing and running their companies and able to easily defer preparing for that sale that will happen sometime down the road. Worry about it later.

Imagine deciding to sell your house today and knowing you have a long list of "to do" items you kept putting off, like fixing the roof, painting the house, repairing the downstairs toilet, upgrading the appliances, and so on and so on. How will failing to address those uncompleted tasks affect the price you will ultimately receive? Negatively, most likely. Clearly your company is worth more than your home – and yet, if you are like most business owners, you have delayed getting ready for the eventual sale of your company. Apparently, business owners need to get their house in order.

What I know for a fact is that one day—I do not know exactly when—but one day, you will no longer own your business. Whether it is voluntarily or involuntarily, horizontally or vertically, at some point in the future, you will exit your business—-I think we can all agree on that. So, if we know that day will arrive, sooner or later, doesn't it make sense to plan for that event?

Failing to properly prepare the business for sale leaves many issues unresolved, things that a buyer will likely discover. Such findings often lead to a lower price, less favorable terms, or the possible termination of your transaction. Getting my clients to embrace what I call the "Seller's Mindset," which we will discuss extensively throughout this book, puts them in the optimal position to achieve the number one goal of every buyer: maximizing the value of the business to receive the highest price and best terms possible.

Over the years, I have been involved in numerous merger and acquisition transactions, mostly on the selling side. In some cases, I was brought in as early as eight years prior to the actual sale; for other transactions, the runway was much shorter, with just a few months to prepare the company. My preference is to be engaged by the owners at least three to five years before the planned sale date, giving ample time to identify and address the major issues that could cause an unsuccessful sale. Once we highlight the areas in your business that pose the greatest risk for a sale (such as a drop in profits, that one large customer who is threatening to take her business elsewhere, the outdated CRM software, and many other issues), we can then address and resolve each issue. This takes time and certainly does not happen overnight.

INTRODUCTION

This book is a compendium of the various transactions that I have been involved in over a 40-plus year career, along with the input of colleagues who are involved in one way or another in the M&A business. There are many lessons I have learned along the way; I know what works and I know what does not work. The purpose of this book is to change your perspective from that of a business owner with no plan of succession to that of a strategist who adopts the Seller's Mindset principles and proactively prepares your company for an eventual sale.

There are three main sections of this book: the Preliminaries, the Planning Phase and the Selling Phase. The first section provides important background information for the rest of the book. For those of you who have not been through the sale of a business, breaking the process down into these three distinct phases will be extremely helpful. Most of what is covered in the Seller's Mindset approach takes place in the planning phase. If you can successfully adopt the Seller's Mindset attitude, you will have paved the way for a smooth selling phase.

Will today be the day you start viewing your business through different lenses? Will you no longer simply think of yourself as a business owner, but instead as a seller who makes decisions with a Seller's Mindset? Will today be the day you start to "Run It Like You'll Sell It"?

THE PRELIMINARIES

CHAPTER 1
THE SELLER'S MINDSET

Henry Ford said, "Before everything else, getting ready is the secret of success."

Growing up, I lived near a neighbor who had the perfect home. The front lawn was a weed-free, perfectly-planted carpet of dichondra, surrounded by constantly manicured shrubbery and trees. The backyard was immaculate, with a beautiful treehouse adorning a large, sprawling oak tree in the middle of the yard. The inside of the house was equally impressive, with pristine walls and perfectly-vacuumed, stain-free carpeting. This house stood out in our lower-middle class neighborhood. It always looked ready for an open house, set to be shown to potential buyers and immediately sold for the asking price. Aside from removing personal belongings, this house was ready for a buyer to move in soon after the closing.

The owners had what I call the "Seller's Mindset," a philosophy of positioning an asset to always be ready to sell. When the time does come for a particular asset to be sold, the owner has few things to do and is able to transact at the best price possible and with favorable terms.

And why not? By having a Seller's Mindset, you have ticked off each item on your "To Do" list by the time you're ready to sell. There are no holes in the roof, peeling paint or stained carpeting. In the case of my neighbor, when they did finally decide to sell their house, they were able to do so at a record price for our neighborhood with a short escrow. Having the Seller's Mindset enabled them to act quickly and eliminate any major issues that might have otherwise jeopardized the sale.

The Seller's Mindset also includes something more: the "Buyer's Perspective." While it is critically important to run your business with the state of mind of always being prepared to sell, that alone may neglect how a buyer will evaluate your business. Without considering how a buyer will react to your business decisions and performance, you are operating in a vacuum that could have negative consequences when you enter into a transaction.

> *Let me offer an example of how I learned the "Buyer's Perspective." During the Goldman Sachs 10,000 Small Businesses Program[1], I learned a valuable lesson on the concept of perspective. In the marketing module, we were asked to describe in one sentence what our companies do. At the time, I owned a high-end home medical equipment retail store and answered the question as follows: "We sell medical supplies and equipment."*
>
> *The "ah ha" moment came when the instructor then shared a saying that forever changed how I thought about my business: "Focus less on what you're selling and more on what your customers are buying."*
>
> *In other words, move away from viewing things through your set of eyes alone, and instead look at things through the lens of the other side, be it a customer, an employee, or a buyer*

---

1 The "Goldman Sachs 10,000 Small Businesses program is an investment to help entrepreneurs create jobs and economic opportunity by providing greater access to education, capital and business support services. To date, more than 9,100 business owners have graduated from the program across all 50 states in the US, Puerto Rico and Washington, D.C." -Per the Goldman Sachs website.

> *of your business. At my store, I realized that our customers were not coming in to buy wheelchairs, scooters, or walkers. From their perspective, they were coming in to buy solutions—they needed to transport a relative more easily to the doctor, for example.*
>
> *To our customers, we were solving problems; the products were simply a means to an end. Learning that allowed us to redirect how we marketed the business and engaged with our customers. This lesson of changing your perspective—from that of yours to that of the other side—is applicable to virtually every aspect of your business and life.*

So, from this point on when we use the term "Seller's Mindset," we will define it as **"the attitude that your business is continually prepared to be sold, addressing all of the issues a buyer would be most concerned about."**

Being aware of the buyer's perspective in preparing your business for sale enables you to evaluate your company's performance from the buyer's point of view, and flips the way you look at your business.

HOW DO YOU IMPLEMENT THE SELLER'S MINDSET?

Well before the anticipated date you plan to sell your company, you start the process of preparing your company for sale in the same way as you would for any other valuable asset, such as your home. It has been said that the day you start your business is the day you should begin to plan to sell it—while that theoretically makes sense, most owners find it difficult to adopt this philosophy, as they're often consumed with the multitude of issues they face while building and running their companies.

> *I know firsthand how difficult it is to start, grow and run a business. I have started several companies (some of which*

were extremely successful, while others I deny being involved in). One such success took over ten years to monetize. In 1999, three businessmen were referred to me to help them raise funds for their Generation X website. I was not that excited about the website, but in their business plan they described a concept that I felt was patentable. They thought I was crazy, but respected me enough to agree to meet with patent counsel who endorsed my idea and urged us to start working on the patent application. After a series of rejections and re-directions over a 10-year period, we were awarded the patent and several additional claims. Once the patent was issued, we discussed the viability of various options for monetizing our efforts. Although I had not yet flushed out the term "the Seller's Mindset", I intuitively knew we had things to do to get our company, specifically the patent, ready for sale. We developed marketing materials and a business plan for the various applications of the patent. If we were going to find a buyer, we had to present to prospects a road map on how our patent would benefit them and make them money. We ended up selling the patent for 7 figures and retained a 25% back-end interest in future proceeds. That was a fun ride!

Each of the companies I started were all-consuming ventures that required the level of focus and attention non-owners will never fully understand. Regardless of that time commitment, requiring myself to adopt the Seller's Mindset helped to prepare me for an exit that placed me in the best possible position to maximize the value of my business.

Having the Seller's Mindset means that every decision you make, from growing your business, to investing in your staff, to improving the quality of your financial statements, is done through the lens of selling your business while accounting for the buyer's perspective. You must constantly

THE SELLER'S MINDSET

ask yourself, "Both on a short-term and a long-term basis, how will this decision affect my earnings and risk—or, in other words, the value of my business?" Place yourself in a buyer's shoes and ask, "How will the buyer view this situation?"

The following chart provides a comparison of how a company employing the Seller's Mindset operates, compared to one that does not:

Issue	Without Seller's Mindset	With Seller's Mindset
Growing Revenues	It is what it is.	Are we achieving linearity? How will a buyer react?
Growing EBITDA	Will try to improve next year.	Are we achieving linearity? How will a buyer react?
Customer Concentration	Looking for new customers.	Must get new customers by a specific date.
Business Valuation	Not aware of current valuation.	Knows current valuation and what drives value.
Risk Assessment	Business is risky in general.	Major risk areas have been identified and addressed.
Telling Your Story	What story?	In full control of your story and how events will affect it.
Recast Analysis	What does it matter?	Recast items are detailed annually.
Prioritized Action Plan	No time for that.	On-going program involving management team and advisors.
Gap Analysis	Worry about that later.	Have met with CPA and wealth advisor to perform analysis.
Due Diligence Prep	Why start now?	Create digital files for key document and analysis.
Buyer Search	No time for that.	Develop a Top 10 list, including info on M&A activity.

Implementing and embracing the Seller's Mindset allows you to focus on doing the things that maximize the value of your business. In Chapter 3, we will discuss the drivers of business value, breaking them down in remarkably simple terms. The two variables to focus on are

RUN IT LIKE YOU'LL SELL IT

growing earnings and reducing risk; addressing these two goals results in a compound benefit to business value. In fact, the affect is so pronounced, we can actually "turbocharge" the value of your business, providing you with the highest price possible at the most favorable terms available when you sell your business.

Failure to run your business with an eye on selling limits your ability to maximize business value. Adopting the Seller's Mindset early on affords you the greatest chance to be successful when the day arrives to actually sell your company. Running your business like you are going to sell it forces you to imagine every day is an "open house," with potential buyers looking closely at all aspects of your business to assess its real value. Getting ready sooner than later—having the Seller's Mindset—lets you eliminate weeds from the lawn and allows you to ensure everything is in order.

The Seller's Mindset means operating your company in a way that builds a lasting organization, with great employees, excellent historical financial performance, long-term customers and vendors, a great reputation, well-maintained equipment, limited negative issues and strong systems and policies.

CHAPTER 2
THE NEED TO BE READY

As with most things you do in life, it makes sense to get ready, prepare, and plan. I have a beautiful vegetable garden that I tend to year-round. At the beginning of each growing season, I spend a lot of time thinking about the vegetables I want to grow, the condition of my soil, changes I might have to make in my irrigation system, etc. Whether it is planting a garden, painting a house, or going on a trip, few would argue the importance of preparation.

When it comes to doing essential things, preparation is critical. And when you think about it, as a business owner, what could be more important than selling your business? It certainly is more crucial than planting a garden, painting a house or going on a trip.

The greatest danger from not being prepared to sell your business—of not adopting the Seller's Mindset—is that you typically do not know when you might decide to sell or when you night need to sell. It's going to happen; you just don't know when.

Author Christopher Bullock wrote The Cobbler of Preston in 1716. In it he says, "'Tis impossible to be sure of anything but Death and Taxes." If Mr. Bullock were alive today, I am certain he would have no issue adding "the sale or transfer of your business." For there will come a day, without a doubt, that you will no longer be the owner of your company.

What might trigger your separation from your business? There are many possibilities. Let's look at the three most common:

- Your intentional decision to sell or transfer ownership of your business
- Reaction to an unsolicited offer to buy your company
- Being forced to sell your business

For the first possibility, you're in the driver's seat when it comes to selling your business. You control the process, including timing, tone and pace. You decide who to talk to and what information to provide, with the ability to present your company in the best possible light. Even if your intended sale date is a few years away, you can still adopt the Seller's Mindset today and begin to get ready for your sale.

Unfortunately, the second and third possibilities noted above are unplanned occurrences that you may find you ill-prepared to present your company in the most favorable position. One day, you may receive an unsolicited yet earnest inquiry to purchase your company. The contact may come from a competitor, a private equity group, or any number of other types of potential buyers. While it may be flattering to receive such an inquiry, the timing can be distractive and inopportune, forcing you to be reactive instead of ready. And, if you have failed to properly prepare your business for a potential sale and are caught "flat-footed" by the inquiring company, it's unlikely you will be in an optimal position to sell—you will most certainly leave money on the table due to failing to prepare appropriately. Oops!

On the positive side, what is the chance of you receiving an unsolicited inquiry from a potential buyer? You tell me. My guess? It is very likely. As I am writing this book, I have a two clients who have been contacted "out of the blue" by interested parties. One is a competitor and the other a private

THE NEED TO BE READY

equity group. While we still have lots of work remaining to get them to the optimal place to approach buyers, both of my clients want to at least test the waters and allow offers to be presented. I get it. Maybe the buyers really want my client's companies. Maybe the buyers will not care about the open areas of risk we have not yet resolved. Maybe. Maybe. Maybe. What I do know is that a buyer will pay more for a company with more earnings and less risk. Period.

Many owners unexpectedly find themselves in situations that force the sale of their business. A variety of negative events can happen with little or no warning, such as an embolism, an affair, the loss of a key employee, a big lawsuit, simple boredom, general malaise or even death. These are the kinds of unforeseen events that can accelerate the need to sell your business. And chances are, you will not be prepared at all. Oops again!

Regardless of the reasons—from the most positive to the most negative—the fact remains that one day you will no longer own your business. The question is this: will you be prepared? The sale of your business is likely one of the most important financial events of your life, and putting your company in the best possible position takes time and planning.

If you are like the typical business owner, your company represents your most valuable asset. You have worked tirelessly hoping for that big payday down the road that will enable you to retire and live the good life. Monetizing all those efforts to get the optimal price and terms is the main goal.

So how do we ensure that you will sell your business at its peak value? The most critical thing is being able to take advantage of time. Like most important things, maximizing the value of your business does not happen overnight, and, if you genuinely want the highest price and the best terms when you sell your business, you have to start today.

I am often asked how much advance time we really need. My simple response is this: the more, the better. Why? In Chapter 5, we discuss the importance of identifying and reducing the major areas of risk in your business. One of the first things to do is to go through a risk evaluation I developed called the "Business Risk Assessment Scorecard"—this is a proprietary tool that examines over 20 areas in your business that affect risk. Knowing that higher risk lowers your business value, the ability to eliminate or lower as many of the identified shortcomings in your business as possible will increase the value of your business. As I have already said, this process does not occur quickly; it takes time.

A good example of why time matters involves the role the owner plays in the business. It is not unusual for the owner to run the company and to be involved in every decision. While that may be reasonable, it does present a risk for a buyer, who will be (logically) concerned that the owner's motivation to work hard will diminish after the sale closes. After all, once the owner receives a big payday and hands over the keys, he or she might not feel motivated to work as hard.

So how do we mitigate that particular risk? We develop a succession plan and explore recruiting someone to take over the day-to-day responsibilities of the owner well before we go to market. If successfully chosen and trained, a hands-on, dedicated general manager (or the managerial equivalent) can directly add value to your business, and, in essence, assist you in preparing it for sale.

That individual may be one of the key employees already in place at the company, or perhaps it may be necessary to look outside the company to find the ideal candidate. In either case, this process takes time. First, training does not happen in a month or two—it requires the benefit of a few business cycles to be most effective. Second, if you do decide to recruit internally, you need time to search for and train the replacement of the promoted employee. And most importantly, if you make a mistake and bring the wrong person on, you have to start over again, while potentially having to repair the damage inflicted by that individual. If you fail to

THE NEED TO BE READY

allocate adequate time for this particular project, you will need to delay selling your company, or be forced to settle for a lower price with potentially inferior terms.

This is just one example of an area to be addressed before the business should be sold. So, knowing how important preparation is in getting the best price and terms for the sale of the business, what are you waiting for?

> *I want to tell you about a former client of mine I will call Steven who started a manufacturing company that grew into the world's largest manufacturer of a well-known consumer product. Not big on planning, Steven hired me to prepare his company for sale. Or at least that is what he told me. From Day One, it was evident that Steven was focused solely on growing his company and had no intention to sell his business in the foreseeable future. I do not regret that he misled me, because working for him exposed me to the most difficult business issues I have ever faced in my career, and gave me examples and stories of how NOT to run a business.*
>
> *Steven had four retail stores in addition to a national chain of independent dealers that sold his products. For the 18-month period that I worked for him, Steven focused a lot of attention on growing the retail business with no real strategic plan for growth. My efforts to upgrade the accounting system, develop detailed policies and procedures, implement internal controls, reduce the level of litigation in the company, and hire several key managers to help take the company to the next level (in other words, to prepare his company for sale) were rejected as unnecessary.*
>
> *Steven had a simple way he measured his success: the balance of his bank account. Unfortunately, Steven thought*

his business was in good shape and did not need to employ any important measurements of the business, including KPIs (key performance indicators), which would have given him advance notice of changes in his business and the industry.

I left Steven after my 18-month contract ran out, although he begged me to stay. I politely explained that I was brought in to do a job that he was not supporting, so I had to leave.

About four years later, I received a phone call from Steven, who told me he had lost a major lawsuit with one of his key vendors, and the result of this lawsuit was that Steven had to surrender ownership to this vendor. He received nothing for his business and lost everything. Steven was living through an event he did not predict or plan for, and it cost him his business.

Had Steven even employed just a few of the items I had proposed to him to prepare his business for an eventual sale, he would likely have avoided the loss of his business. Had he implemented internal controls and better financial reporting, he likely could even have avoided the lawsuit that cost him his business. Unfortunately for Steven and his family, the lack of preparation cost them millions of dollars.

Steven failed to adopt a Seller's Mindset. He failed to take seriously the risks of not planning for a future that had the potential to cause his company to implode. Steven was so consumed with running his business that he failed to plan for the sale of his business—instead, he lost it all.

You do not want to be like Steven. In your business, the need to be ready is likely very real, and the results of not being prepared could be catastrophic. Whether planned or not, you already know that one day you will cease being the owner. What is the chance of a major, negative event happening to you one day? Higher than you might realize.

THE NEED TO BE READY

The time to get ready is now; if you are not planning for the eventual sale of your business, you are putting in jeopardy perhaps the most valuable asset you own.

> **BEST PRACTICE**
>
> Put time on your side. Start preparing today...preferably this morning.

CHAPTER 3
A PRIMER ON BUSINESS VALUE

Let's spend some time discussing business value. Why is this important? I have never met a business owner who said to me, "Let's not try to get the very best price and terms for my business." However, the topic of business valuation can be very complex, with terminology like discounted cash flow, enterprise value, weighted-average cost of capital, and terminal rates. Forget all of that—I like to keep it extremely simple.

In its simplest form, the value of your business can be measured using a straightforward formula with just two variables:

$$\text{Business Value} = \frac{\text{Cash Flow}}{\text{Risk}}$$

Business Value equals Cash Flow, divided by Risk

Quite simply, that is all that matters: **The value of a business is computed by the amount of cash flow it generates, offset by the amount of risk present in the business.** Focus on those two variables and watch your business value grow.

Cash flow is usually measured as EBITDA, which is an abbreviation for earnings before interest, taxes, depreciation and amortization.

What is risk? **I define risk as "any aspect of the company that reduces the ability to predict the future."** Business risk can present itself in numerous ways. Whether the company has issues like sporadic earnings history, customer concentration issues, or high employee turnover (to name a few), the presence of too much risk in a business (as perceived by the buyer) will have a negative impact on the value of the business because it makes it more difficult for the buyer to predict the future. From the formula above, as the denominator (risk) increases, business value decreases. Conversely, as risk is reduced, business value grows. That is why it is so important to identify and reduce the risk factors in your business.

The following chart illustrates the relationship between risk and value:

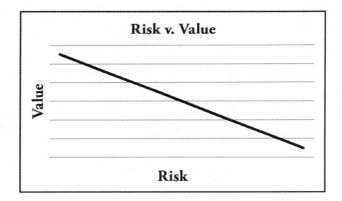

As we move along the risk spectrum, from low to high, value decreases.

Unfortunately, risk is difficult to measure. So instead, a multiple of cash flow is used to determine business value, as shown in the following formula:

$$\text{Business Value} = \text{Cash Flow} \times \text{Multiple}$$

A PRIMER ON BUSINESS VALUE

The follow chart depicts the relationship between risk and the multiple:

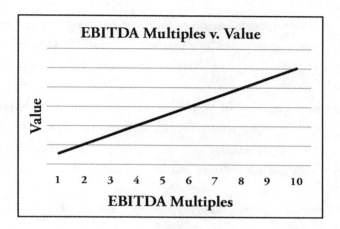

As EBITDA multiples rise, so does value.

From the two formulas for business value shown here, you can see the inverse relationship between risk and the multiple. But why does the idea of having lower risk yield a higher multiple? What are the dynamics at play?

Take a company that has a lot of risk in its business, such as unreliable financial statements, customer concentration issues, an owner who is too integral to the business or massive workers' compensation claims. That business has a more difficult time predicting what next month's or next year's revenues and profits will be, and the inability to predict with some degree of accuracy makes it difficult to plan (e.g., how much operating capacity, raw materials, or staffing levels the business will need). On the other hand, a company with lower risk levels, such as linear financial performance, excellent IT systems and protected intellectual property, can more easily and accurately predict the future.

It all comes down to predictability—reduce the risk and you improve the predictability. And that is why buyers are willing to pay more for a lower risk company (i.e., pay a higher multiple). They have a higher degree of confidence in predicting future operating performance. Note to self: lower your risk.

Determining an exact earnings multiple is part art and part science. Valuation experts can provide guidance on multiples based on recent transactions in your industry. Many buyers like to stay within a range of multiples, making an offer usually calculated by a specific multiple based on their perception of your company's specific risk determined by how the buyer views numerous factors within your company. Getting a buyer to improve their valuation of your company involves being able to communicate the various things you have done over the years to mitigate business risk.

Combining this lower risk with strong, consistently-growing earnings makes your company more attractive to buyers because they can predict your future with a higher degree of certainty, resulting in higher valuations—the result of "turbocharging" the value of your business.

Now, before you start to email me that this explanation of business value is too simple and that many buyers use a much more complex approach to valuing target companies, I concede that is true. However, regardless of whether a buyer uses a complex valuation model involving esoteric computations and scenarios or a simpler approach described in this chapter, it all comes down to earnings and risk. Life is complicated enough. Business valuation doesn't have to be.

Embrace the Seller's Mindset and focus on those initiatives that grow EBITDA and reduce risk.

> **BEST PRACTICE**
>
> Have your business valued today by a professional valuation expert, using recent sales data for your industry.

CHAPTER 4
THE VALUE QUARTERBACK

Later in this book, we will talk about building your team of trusted advisors, including your accountant, wealth advisor, and attorney. Each trusted advisor plays a critical role in guiding you throughout the process to ensure a successful outcome. **Just as every good football team needs a quarterback, you should consider engaging the services of a professional who will take the lead and guide you through the process of selling your company, from the planning phase through the selling phase, and even the post-close phase.**

In choosing such an individual to be your exit quarterback, you should consider retaining the services of an individual with extensive experience in growing and running companies, and in maximizing (even turbocharging) their value and in the mergers and acquisition field. This individual should have a comprehensive understanding of the drivers of value—namely cash flow and risk—and be able to determine how to best apply that knowledge to your company. I call this individual the "Value Quarterback."

Most small- to mid-sized companies do not have the resources for this type of person inside the company. Appointing the controller, vice president of finance, or CFO to this role is often ineffective, as this individual will more than likely not have the time or experience required to effectively oversee the many aspects that need to be addressed in preparing the business for sale. If you want to be successful, you will likely have to go outside your company for help.

In selecting a Value Quarterback, I suggest seeking out an individual with the Certified Exit Planning Advisor® ("CEPA") designation, which was created by the Exit Planning Institute for individuals who successfully complete their "…executive MBA-style program that trains and certifies qualified professional advisors in the field of exit planning."

While as of March 1, 2021, there are only 2,100 CEPA professionals worldwide, not all individuals with the CEPA designation play the role of the Value Quarterback. Many CEPA professionals are wealth advisors or CPAs who received their CEPA designations to be conversant in the area of exit planning, but who do not work with business owners on the many details of business sale preparedness, value maximization, and transactional completion.

As a business owner, you are probably particularly good at running your own company, maybe you are even considered an expert in your industry. But when it comes to preparing your company for sale, you likely have little or no experience. Find someone who knows what it takes to prepare your business for an eventual sale, who does this work full time, and who has invested the resources to be the expert.

In my consulting firm, The PrimeMark Group™, we work with successful companies to maximize their business value in preparation for an eventual sale or ownership transfer. We play the role of the Value Quarterback from start to finish. Some of the services we perform include:

Initial Meeting	Risk Assessment	Prioritized Action Plan	Financial Analysis	Recast Analysis
Valuation Analysis	Telling Your Story	Growing EBITDA	Gap Analysis	Due Diligence Prep
Marketing Your Company	Letter of Intent	Due Diligence	Definitive Agreements	Post Closing

THE VALUE QUARTERBACK

- **Initial Meeting with Owner(s):** Each company has its own unique features and characteristics, while each owner has his or her own specific goals and issues that need to be discussed, analyzed and addressed to ensure a successful outcome. Our initial meeting will provide the opportunity to get to know each other and to see if we can add significant value to your process. During this discussion, we encourage you to be as honest and complete as possible—if there are any land mines out there, they will be discovered during the due diligence phase.
- **Business Risk Assessment:** As described previously, risk is one of the two primary variables in determining the value of your business. Using our proprietary "Business Risk Assessment Scorecard" (described in Chapter 5, we identify the areas in your business that pose the greatest risk from a buyer's perspective. We issue a written report with our recommendations to address those identified risk areas. Next, we meet to review our findings and make necessary adjustments.
- **Prioritized Action Plan:** Once we agree on the risk areas to address, we'll create your "Prioritized Action Plan" to address your areas of risk, including the priority level of each item, intended outcomes, required resources, timelines (initial, mid-term and final), project lead, team members and outside resources. The "Prioritized Action Plan" is a fluid document, constantly being revised. We typically work in 90-day sprints to ensure deadlines are met and that progress is made, while being mindful to avoid making this process burdensome on you or your staff.
- **Financial Analysis:** Your financial statements will be carefully scrutinized by any potential buyer. We perform a comprehensive review of your historical financial statements to fully understand your performance over the last few years, carefully noting those areas that are inconsistent or that will cause a buyer concern in

forecasting the future. We will review your budget data (including variance analysis), and your forecast, if available. Finally, we will discuss opportunities to grow EBITDA as part of the overall strategy of maximizing the value of your business.

- **Recast Analysis:** Many companies incur expenses that will not continue after a sale or that occur just one time, such as a rare lawsuit. To be able to eventually present a potential buyer with accurate information, we analyze these items to determine how best to properly present a buyer with a post-transaction account of EBITDA, upon which it will base its offer price. We also develop and maintain a detailed, trailing 12-month analysis for the income statement, to gauge in a timely manner any changes in recast EBITDA.
- **Valuation Analysis:** As a starting point to gauge valuation growth, a top-side valuation analysis will be prepared. The report is not a lengthy, traditional valuation analysis, but will document a range of EBITDA multiples that are transactionally-based to serve as a benchmark for future valuation tracking.
- **Telling Your Story:** Overlooked by many advisors, "telling your story" is a critically important part of how you distinguish yourself from other sellers that the buyer may be considering. What sets you apart from the competition? What is your sustainable, competitive advantage? The story you tell today will likely change overtime. We will help you write it and update it, so that when the time comes to meet with potential buyers, your story is ready to be told.
- **Growing EBITDA:** In addition to finding ways to reduce risk in your business, we also look for opportunities to grow EBITDA. Beginning with revenues, we'll review your sales plan, if available, and explore areas to increase your customer base as well as your reach within your existing base of business. We will concurrently

review your expenses to identify potential savings. This is discussed in more detail in Chapter 6.

- **Gap Analysis:** There are three gaps to be analyzed to ensure that the proceeds you receive from the sale of your business on an after-tax basis are sufficient—together with other financial assets you own—to provide you with the cash flow you will need to live on post-close. We work with your CPA and wealth advisor (if available) to perform the gap analysis.
- **Due Diligence Preparation:** For those sellers who want to be in a "ready mode" for a potential transaction, we coordinate the gathering of key documents that will be required in due diligence, including historical financial statements and tax returns, tax audit information, revenue analysis by source type, the organization chart, employment agreements, employee handbook, employee list, benefit plan data and filings, insurance schedules and loss runs, top customer and vendor lists, customer and vendor contracts, intellectual property lists, fixed asset lists, litigation information, IT equipment list (including LAN/WAN diagram), safety-related information, related party transaction information, to name a few.
- **Marketing Your Company:** When you are ready to start the process of marketing your business, we meet with you to ensure we fully understand your goals and intended outcomes. The impact of all of the work outlined above is to ensure you have properly prepared your business for sale, enabling us to present your company in the best possible light. Typically, we prepare a one page "teaser" document that describes your business but does not identify it. This document is sent to potential buyers that we (as a team) identify as potential buyers.

You likely already know who your buyer will be, or at least who the top three possibilities are. You know who your competition is, and you know who the active buyers in your industry are. We will supplement that important knowledge with market research as well as our contacts to identify the most logical buyers, taking into account your goals and objectives, as well as your desired timeline.

From the one page "teaser" document, we prepare a longer document (typically 15–30 pages), which describes your business in more detail to provide qualified potential buyers with sufficient information to submit offers. This longer document is only provided to qualified parties whom you have approved and who execute a non-disclosure agreement. Please note that sensitive information will initially only be provided in a redacted format. We field any questions and requests from this select group and move the process forward to enable submission of offers, in the form of a letter of intent.

- **Letter of Intent Negotiation:** Once potential buyers present their letters of intent, we work with you to review the offer prices and proposed terms. We analyze the various offers to ensure they cover all of the seller's key deal points to prevent major issues once the definitive agreements are drafted. We work with the select group of potential buyers to make appropriate revisions in an attempt to resolve valuation and term differences. At this stage, our goal is to have you and one of the potential buyers execute the negotiated letter of intent and move into the due diligence phase.
- **Due Diligence:** From the information gathered during the due diligence preparation, we will open a dedicated virtual data room ("VDR") as a secure location to provide the buyer with requested documents and analysis. We will review the buyer's document request list with the seller to determine the availability of the requested documents, and our willingness to provide the requested items. We will field questions from the buyer's team and act as a buffer for the seller.

- **The Definitive Agreements:** In conjunction with seller's legal counsel, we will review the various agreements prepared by the buyer. Our comments, while not meant to be legal advice or to replace the work of seller's legal counsel, will be business-based. We will also assist you in retaining proper counsel for your sale, if needed.
- **Post-Closing:** We will be available after the closing to assist the seller on post-close matters, such as holdbacks, earn-out, and working capital true-ups.

Over the years, you have likely assembled a team of trusted advisors to provide you with guidance in making important decisions, including your outside CPA, attorney, banker, and insurance agent. These professionals will likely play critical roles in preparing your company for sale. We will provide input for you regarding your trusted advisors, ensuring that you have the appropriate level of advice for selling your business.

Preparing a business for sale, and successfully completing the transaction, require the skills of trained professionals with years of valuable experience. Engaging a Value Quarterback professional from the beginning and through the consummation of the sale will provide you with the consistency needed to ensure the most successful outcome.

> **BEST PRACTICE**
>
> Seek out the services of a qualified Value Quarterback as soon as possible.

THE PLANNING PHASE

CHAPTER 5
ASSESSING RISK

As part of the Planning Process, it is important to identify those areas in the business that pose risks for a potential buyer. The seller must ask, **"Which parts of my company will a buyer have concerns about?"** Or **"What reservations about my company's future might a buyer bring up?"** These areas of risk must be identified and addressed before taking a company to market, or the value of the business will suffer. Referring back to the earlier analogy of selling a home, the presence of poor landscaping, chipped paint, or stained carpeting will all negatively impact the buyer's perception of the house—and therefore the value of the offer. Your business is no different.

The time to identify and address your areas of risk must start now. Pinpointing the areas of risk in your business will not take that much time, but resolving them likely will. To help with this, I have developed the "Business Risk Assessment Scorecard," an assessment tool that examines over 20 areas of a company to determine where risk is present in the business—risk that will be viewed unfavorably by the buyer.

Among the areas we explore are:

- Financial performance
- Tax matters
- Personnel and labor relations

RUN IT LIKE YOU'LL SELL IT

- Deal structure and valuation analysis
- Customers
- Vendors

I use the Business Risk Assessment Scorecard for all new clients as an excellent tool to determine where the problem areas exist in their businesses. From the list of the categories shown above, the risks that are identified span the entire business and can include such items as errors in the financial statements, an owner who is too important to the business, customer concentration, a nagging lawsuit, undocumented intellectual property, or corporate books and records that have not been kept up-to-date.

The perspective I like to give my (selling) clients is that of the buyer. For example, I might ask my client, "How would you react as a buyer if the selling company had one customer that accounted for 70% of its revenues? Would it concern you?" Of course it would. "Would it affect the price you would pay for the business?" Definitely. We review all of the identified areas of risk in a similar manner and develop solutions for each area of risk.

The Business Risk Assessment Scorecard takes about two hours to complete. The results are analyzed and scored, based on the responses received to the various questions. An overall score is tabulated and a summary report to the client is produced, which identifies the major areas to be addressed. A recommendation for how to deal with each area of risk is also presented. The report, in draft format, is presented to the client for discussion and modification. From this report, the "Prioritized Action Plan" is created as a working document to itemize the various risk areas to resolve. It includes information such as intended outcomes, required resources, timelines, the project lead, team members, and outside resources. Revisions are made regularly with input from the team.

I recently took a new client through my Business Risk Assessment Scorecard process. Although it only takes about two hours, it is still two hours of precious time that the business owner could be using on other aspects

ASSESSING RISK

of the business. When we concluded with the questionnaire, I apologized to my client that it had taken so long. He responded, "Are you kidding? I learned so many things about my business I never knew before. Thank you!"

In Chapter 3, we defined business value as cash flow divided by risk, with business value having an inverse relationship to risk. In other words, as risk increases, business value decreases. Or, in more positive terms, as we reduce risk, business value will go up. That is why risk is so important—our ability to identify and eliminate the risky areas of your business is guaranteed to have a positive impact on the value of your company.

Said another way, as we are able to lower the risk in your business, the multiple will grow, yielding a higher business value. So perhaps the easiest way to understand risk is to realize that, as risk goes down, multiples go up, yielding an increase in the value of your company. If you are hoping to put more money in the bank from selling your business, focus on risk. Period.

Why should I start now preparing for the sale of my business? Because it takes time. Reducing customer concentration, for example, may require a large effort on the part of the company and it might not produce results for a long while. Having to make staffing changes or additions will also likely consume sizable amounts of time. Failing to address these areas of risk early on puts you in jeopardy of owning an ill-prepared company that, for one reason or another, you may find yourself having to sell quickly. I like to avoid those types of situations, and I'm sure you would too.

Identifying and addressing risk early on enables you to adopt the Seller's Mindset, being in a constant state of readiness with no open, major issues remaining when you go to sell your company.

> **BEST PRACTICE**
>
> Start the process of assessing your risk now, while time is on your side.

CHAPTER 6
GROWING EBITDA

In Chapter 3, we broke down the complex aspect of business value into two simple variables that allow any business to maximize business value.

$$\text{Business Value} = \frac{\text{Cash Flow}}{\text{Risk}}$$

Business Value equals Cash Flow (EBITDA), divided by Risk

A good deal of this book addresses the concept of reducing risk as a means to maximizing business value. In this chapter, we will focus on ways to grow cash flow or EBITDA. Our two areas of focus are revenues and expenses.

Revenues: Consistently growing revenues not only help to improve EBITDA, but also give a buyer confidence about forecasting a company's future performance. As part of your annual budgeting process, you should develop a detailed sales plan that is forecasted to yield healthy revenue gains each year. The development of such a plan should be done with input from your entire sales staff: ask them to identify opportunities for their top 20 accounts, with detail estimates for each customer by product type or item, if relevant.

RUN IT LIKE YOU'LL SELL IT

A former boss of mine once explained the two main ways to grow revenues. He said, **"You sell old products to new people or new products to old people."** In other words, you can increase revenues by expanding your customer base, or by getting your existing customers to buy more items on your line card. This is a simple way to explain to your salesforce how to improve their sales results. One thing missing from this bit of wisdom is growing revenues by raising prices, a concept foreign to most salespeople. Let me share with you a story about pricing with a former client of mine.

> *Many years ago, I was retained buy a public warehousing company that was in financial distress and was hoping to avoid having to file for bankruptcy. Initially, I spent a lot of time understanding what drove the business. I learned that while the company was operating at full capacity and was seemingly well-run, with a clean and beautifully-organized warehouse, it nevertheless had been unable to turn a profit. In terms of cost savings, I concluded that operating expenses had been trimmed as far as they could without negatively impacting the company's service level. I then asked for a meeting with the two owners to share my findings and to make my sole recommendation.*
>
> *I explained to them that the best solution I could come up with to increase their cash flow was for them to approach their top 15 customers and ask for a rate increase of at least 15%. I had determined that if they were able to get this from at least half of those customers, then we could save the business. My client hesitated, telling me that if they were to do what I recommended, they would go out of business because they would lose those customers to a company offering a lower price. I explained to my customer that if they did not do what I had*

recommended, they would go out of business anyway. What did they have to lose?

I returned to the company two weeks later for a briefing on how their meetings went with their customers. Both of the owners were grinning from ear-to-ear—they told me that they met with all 15 customers and that every one of them agreed to the 15% increase, with the exception of their largest customer, who accounted for 25% of their business. They explained to me that this customer in particular would not give them a 15% increase, but instead told them to raise their rates by 20%. This customer admitted that my client's company provided services to them at a level unmatched by any other warehousing company.

My client's company was successful in avoiding bankruptcy, but more importantly learned something valuable about their reputation and their benefit to their customers. For your company, knowing your value to your customers is critical. Encourage your sales staff to learn how important you are to key customers, who can also educate you on their other suppliers, such as your competitors.

Require your sales staff to also provide to you their estimates of gross margin by customer, along with any special resources they might need for a particular customer to achieve their sales goal. Gather these individual plans early enough for them to be presented, reviewed, and revised, if needed. Consider having your sales staff produce a "target" plan and a "stretch" plan to illustrate potential revenues if all the stars line up.

These are just a few of the ways an owner can improve their company's sales strategy. Once your sales plan is completed, share it with each member of your sales staff, so that everyone is aware of what is expected of them.

Expenses: In an effort to grow EBITDA, a careful examination of your expenses may yield some ideas. Start first with your largest expense items, which will be different based on your industry. If you are a manufacturer or a distributor, review your cost of goods sold to determine if there are any cost savings available. If you are happy with your existing suppliers, approach them with the possibility of signing a long-term contract for a lower price. Retain the Seller's Mindset to determine what impact such a contract might have if you decide to sell the business. If you do enter into a contract of this type, ensure that it is transferable and terminable under certain circumstances, such as a change of ownership of the business.

For payroll expenses, study your employee list to determine if any cuts can be made. However, remember that the Seller's Mindset attitude does not mean to eliminate necessary expenditures. If you do have excess personnel on your payroll, however, consider reducing this extra expense as a way to increase your bottom line. Businesses often carry underperforming employees for a long time—this exercise may provide the impetus to make necessary changes, with or without a sale.

Perform a similar review of other payroll-related items, such as employee benefits, training and workers' compensation insurance. Special care must be taken not to eliminate items that will have a negative effect on your personnel. In the case of workers' compensation insurance, it pays to shop around with different carriers, especially industry-specific insurance companies that may be able to provide lower base rates.

Other types of insurance are also another potential area to reduce expenses. Every few years, you should shop your general liability and other business-related insurance policies with other brokers to ensure that you are paying the lowest possible prices for your insurance coverage. This review should not just include premiums, but should also look at limits and coverage to see if there are any savings available.

GROWING EBITDA

Payroll- and insurance-related expenses are just a couple of examples of expenses that could be reduced as a way to improve EBITDA. Review each of your expenses to determine if you can make any reductions without negatively impacting the core of your operations.

> **BEST PRACTICE**
>
> Carefully review your income statement to identify opportunities to grow EBITDA.

CHAPTER 7
A CASE STUDY ON TURBOCHARGING BUSINESS VALUE

In the last two chapters, we discussed risk and EBITDA as the two variables that determine value. The case study that follows will illustrate the impact on the value of a business of both reducing risk and growing EBITDA, resulting in a compound impact on value, or what I like to call "Turbocharging Business Value".

The following assumptions are used for the case study:

>   Revenues $50,000,000
>   EBITDA $4,500,000
>   EBITDA as a % of Revenues 9.00%
>   EBITDA Multiple 4.00
>   Estimated Business Value $18,000,000

Using these assumptions, the impact of improving EBITDA on the estimated value of the business is analyzed; no changes in the EBITDA multiple will be assumed for this specific analysis.

The first column is the "Current" level of performance, while the next column ("Better") assumes an improvement in EBITDA of $1.5 million. The final column ("Best") increases EBITDA by another $1.5 million, or $3.0 million above the current EBITDA level of $4.5 million. While this analysis assumes improvement only in the dollar amount of EBITDA, with no improvement in the EBITDA multiple, the impact of just growing EBITDA is still rather dramatic, with business value growing from $18 million to $24 million in the "Better" case scenario, and from $18 million to $30 million in the "Best" case scenario.

	Improve EBITDA Only		
	Current	Better	Best
EBITDA	$4,500,000	$6,000,000	$7,500,000
EBITDA Multiple	4.00	4.00	4.00
Estimated Value	$18,000,000	$24,000,000	$30,000,000
Value Improvement		$6,000,000	$12,000,000
		33%	67%

The next analysis in this case study determines the impact on business value from just lowering risk or, stated in different terms, from increasing the EBITDA multiple. Starting with the current EBITDA multiple of 4.0, enough risk will assume to be eliminated to grow the EBITDA multiple to 5.5. Without figuring in any improvement in EBITDA—i.e., keeping it flat at $4.5 million—in the "Better" case scenario the impact of growing the EBITDA multiple to 5.5 grows the value of the business from $18.00 million to $24.75, a 38% improvement in value. As shown in the "Best" case scenario, risk is then assumed to be reduced even further, resulting in a higher EBITDA multiple from 5.5 to 7.0. Business value improves $13.5 million, or 75% from the current level.

A CASE STUDY ON TURBOCHARGING BUSINESS VALUE

Improve EBITDA Multiple Only			
	Current	Better	Best
EBITDA	$4,500,000	$4,500,000	$4,500,000
EBITDA Multiple	4.00	5.50	7.00
Estimated Value	$18,000,000	$24,750,000	$31,500,000
Value Improvement		$6,750,000	$13,500,000
		38%	75%

The first table assumes improvements in EBITDA alone, with no corresponding increases in the EBITDA multiples, while the second table illustrates growth in just the EBITDA multiples, without any enhancements in the EBITDA levels. The analysis is presented this way to isolate the variables; in real life, such analysis is impractical, with the potential for rising EBITDA and EBITDA multiple occurring simultaneously. The following table illustrates the impact on the value of a business in the midst of growing EBITDA and EBITDA multiples.

Improve EBITDA and EBITDA Multiple Simultaneously			
	Current	Better	Best
EBITDA	$4,500,000	$6,000,000	$7,500,000
EBITDA Multiple	4.00	5.50	7.00
Estimated Value	$18,000,000	$33,000,000	$52,500,000
Value Improvement		$15,000,000	$34,500,000
		83%	192%

Taking the assumptions in the first two tables and combining them shows the compound effect of concurrently growing EBITDA and the EBITDA multiples. In the "Better" scenario, increasing EBITDA by $1.5 million, while also lowering risk enough to grow the EBITDA multiple from 4.0 to 5.5, yields a $15 million (83%) increase in value. Even more dramatic is the "Best" case scenario, where EBITDA improves from $4.5 million to $7.0 million, while significant changes to risk are implemented to enable an improvement in the EBITDA multiple from 4.0 to 7.0, resulting in an overall growth in business value of $34.5 million, or 192%. Where I come from, that is real money. In fact, I refer to this as "Turbocharging".

While this degree of improvement may be impractical for your business, being able to achieve some degree of growth in EBITDA and EBITDA multiple will positively impact your business value.

> **BEST PRACTICE**
>
> Focus both on risk and on growing EBITDA to get the turbocharge effect on the value of your business.

CHAPTER 8
TELLING YOUR STORY

If you have ever been in a position to raise money, look for a job, or otherwise attract the attention of others, you most likely developed an "elevator pitch" for the purposes of informing others succinctly and quickly about what you are trying to accomplish. This elevator pitch assumes you do not have a lot of time (say, the length of the average elevator ride) to convince the other party to listen to what you are about to tell them.

When you take your company to market to be sold, you will likely not be limited to a brief elevator pitch when meeting with potential buyers, although the ability to describe your business in a concise manner will be extremely helpful. If a buyer is unable to quickly understand what your company does, it will be quite easy for the buyer to move on to the next opportunity.

Aside from merely being able to attract someone's attention in a short period of time, you should start to focus on the concept of "Telling Your Story." This is where you are able to educate the buyer about what drives your company, how you face adversity, how you stack up against your competitors, what your track record has been, where you are headed, what sets you apart and makes your company what it is, what your sustainable competitive advantage is, what your company culture is, and how fantastic your employees are.

RUN IT LIKE YOU'LL SELL IT

"Telling Your Story" is your chance to gain the attention of potential buyers, impressing and intriguing them enough to want to learn even more about your business. The story you tell excites the buyer, eliciting questions and a desire to gain a deeper understanding of your business. The more a potential buyer wants to know about your company, the more interested they are in buying it.

Your "story" will inevitably change over time, as events and circumstances present themselves to you and your company. What is most important in "Telling Your Story" is having a deep awareness that the actions you take will craft the story you can tell.

> *Let me offer an example. When COVID-19 first hit in early 2020, most companies suffered severe, negative consequences. Revenues plunged and cash flow evaporated. As it became readily evident that we were not going to quickly emerge from the effects of the pandemic, I was asked by business owners how 2020 would affect their business valuations. My answer to each of them was the same: It all depends on how you tell your story. If by the fourth quarter of 2020, your business began to show recovery, or even perhaps grew from the fourth quarter of 2019, then the negative impact from earlier in the year would likely be overlooked by a potential buyer. If, however, your business was still suffering at the end of 2020, with no foreseeable recovery, then the story you are able to tell is not a good one, and your valuation will likely go down.*

The elements which become part of your story will be unique to your business. For some it might be the opening of a new factory, while for others it could be the departure of a key employee. Perhaps you lost a key customer, or discovered some valuable intellectual property. How you deal

TELLING YOUR STORY

with the negative events, and how many positive elements you can count, will be woven into your story. **The important element here is to be ever aware that you one day will be "Telling Your Story."**

The timing of that "one day" is important: you may conclude that it is best to delay selling your company—and therefore having to tell your story—until your story improves. Let me share another example:

> *One of my clients had a customer that accounted for nearly 60% of total revenues. In spite of my regular warnings to my client that this customer concentration issue presented a high degree of risk, the company was too busy to address the issue by bringing on board other large accounts. As my client had been warned, the day eventually came when that large customer decided to take its business elsewhere, nearly putting my client out of business. Had my client decided to sell the business at that time, the story would have been negative and not well-received by a buyer. However, I advised my client to delay a potential sale and address the revenue shortfall instead.*
>
> *Over the course of the next six months, my client and the sales team were able to procure several new accounts, which in total made up for more than the lost revenue. The effect of these efforts was to not only eliminate the previous customer concentration issue, but also to grow revenues and profits. These actions enabled us to turn a negative story into a positive one, and allowed my client to present potential buyers with a path toward higher cash flow and lower risk. In other words, a higher business value.*

As part of the Seller's Mindset approach, starting from Day One, begin to craft your story and be mindful that whatever happens at your business

RUN IT LIKE YOU'LL SELL IT

will impact your story. As events occur—good and bad—your story will be impacted by your reaction to them. Always know that one day you will be "Telling Your Story" to potential buyers who will react to your story, favorably or not.

Which story will you tell?

> **BEST PRACTICE**
>
> Your story is a fluid one. Write out five sentences about the story you will tell today. Update every six months.

CHAPTER 9
FINANCIAL DATA

One of the main reasons a buyer spends so much time pouring through the seller's historical financial data is to determine the future performance of the target company and to ascertain the true value of the business. I tell my clients that **the buyer is not purchasing present or past performance, but is certainly going to pay a lot of attention to analyzing this information and gauging where the company is headed. After all, the buyer is purchasing the future of your company.**

I know many owners do not believe their financial statements are that important and spend little time reviewing them. This practice must change immediately; your financial statements are one of the best measurements of your company's financial condition, and, in a sense, "tell the story" of your company. And it is your financial statements that the buyer will review in detail and use as reference points in determining the value of your business.

> *Let me share with you a story about financial reports. I had a client who hired my firm many years ago to identify ways to improve profitability and cash flow. While my client did glance over his financial statements each month, he rarely reviewed the many reports deposited into his inbox each day by the IT department. One day, he and I were brainstorming*

about ways to improve financial performance, and I described to him a report I wanted to be able to review. He lamented that he too wished he had such a report, and that it would help him run his business more efficiently. He called up the head of his IT department and explained what we wanted. The IT person politely replied, "Are you referring to the report I put in your inbox each morning?" Sheepishly, my client ended the call and found the "magic" report. It was there all along, not even being looked at!

As the owner, you must be cognizant of your financial performance at all times. In the previous chapter, we discussed the importance of "Telling Your Story." What does your financial performance tell the buyer about your story? Is your historical track record easy to follow, or is it confusing? Even before you meet a potential buyer, you must try to manage your financial results to maximize the quality of your story. Of course, not all events are manageable, and negative performance will probably occur. But you still must be able to manage it, emerge from it, and prevent its recurrence. Easier said than done? Perhaps. But the benefit of starting early is affording yourself the time to recover from negative performance and minimize the impact it might have on the value of your business when you go to market.

In preparing a company for an eventual sale, I produce a package of information for qualified potential buyers, including summary, historical financial statements for the past three years. The income statement includes a top-side analysis of recast add backs (discussed in more detail later in this chapter). I also pull together descriptive information about the company that will serve as important narrative for a package to be presented to potential buyers. In the time leading up to marketing the business, this package must be revised regularly, as changes occur with your company.

FINANCIAL DATA

Even prior to producing the LOI and entering into due diligence, the buyer will attempt to get as much financial information about the seller as possible. It is a delicate balancing act—on the one hand providing the buyer with sufficient information to be able to make a meaningful offer, the terms of which hopefully will not materially change during due diligence, and on the other hand preventing the disclosure of too much information, too early on. After all, if the potential buyer decides not to proceed, or they offer an unacceptable price, you want to make sure you have not provided too much information, especially if that buyer is a competitor. For example, it is not unusual for a buyer to request a list of your top 10 or 20 customers for the past few years. This information is highly confidential and should only be provided to a potential buyer, prior to a LOI, in a redacted format, even if you have executed a non-disclosure agreement.

Signing a non-disclosure agreement is a "feel-good" document that acknowledges the confidential aspect of the seller's disclosure document but provides little help if your data ends up in the wrong hands, especially if you are dealing with more than one potential buyer at a time. Regardless, you should always execute a non-disclosure agreement with any potential buyer. If any buyer refuses to sign one, take that as an early warning sign of future issues and walk away!

Let's spend a few minutes discussing the concept of "non-linearity". Knowing that the buyer is reviewing your financial statements for the purpose of determining future performance, it is beneficial to have as much linearity in your historical results as possible. Now I know this is not necessarily easy to accomplish, but it is critical to present financial statements to a potential buyer that have consistency to them.

Consider the following example of two different companies:

> Company A had a 15% revenue growth for each of the last three years and recast EBITDA growth for each of the last three years of 20%. Company B had a much less consistent

record, with revenue growth of 8% three years ago, followed by revenue decrease the next year of 12%, and revenue growth last year of 15%. Company B's EBITDA pattern was even more inconsistent, with growth when revenue fell and a pullback when revenue grew.

After careful financial analysis a buyer can easily forecast future financial performance for Company A. But where does a buyer go with the volatile, historical results of Company B? Not far. That uncertainty causes a buyer to hedge their bet by being conservative with valuation and terms, because the buyer will view this inconsistency as risk, and higher risk lowers business value.

As a seller, it is critical that you run the business with an eye on consistency and predictability. Understanding that one day you will have to tell your story to a buyer should be a guide in running the business. Now I understand that this is unrealistic for many buyers and many companies. Inconsistencies happen; the real world is not neat and does not always result in consistent performance. I get it!

The point here is that the more linear your historical performance is, the easier it will be for a buyer to predict future performance and to pay you a higher price. Often there is a "linear" story buried in non-linear results—in my experience, there are cases where the results can be presented on a pro-forma basis to isolate those unusual events causing non-linearity.

The accuracy of any information provided to a potential buyer is critically important. Internally-produced, compiled financial statements are viewed cautiously by most buyers, requiring additional work in due diligence, and potentially causing the need for an adjustment in pricing and terms.

In providing potential buyers with the requested financial information, special care should be taken to ensure that it is acceptable to delay the

FINANCIAL DATA

dispensation of such information, if that extra time is needed to ensure accuracy. Inaccurate information will likely be flushed out during due diligence and can catch a seller off guard as they try to explain the errors themselves, and will likely result in a negative adjustment to the purchase price. That is something I try desperately to avoid.

In Chapter 22, we discuss the Quality of Earnings ("QOE") report. Sellers who do not want to go through the expense of a QOE report should consider increasing the scrutiny over their internal financial statements by having them reviewed or audited by a reputable accounting firm. Buyers will look more favorably upon reviewed or audited financial statements.

To ensure you do not leave money on the table, let's discuss what makes up recast addbacks. **Remember that the goal is to provide a potential buyer with a pathway to understand the level of future cash flow the company is capable of producing.** Therefore, the addbacks are critical to eliminate those expenses that will not be present once the buyer takes over. Before you have signed a LOI, it is too early in the negotiation to provide the buyer with the detail of these add backs, yet it is important to make sure you have the sufficient detail to back these numbers up. The buyer will carefully scrutinize the recast adjustments during the due diligence phase.

There are four categories of addbacks to consider:

- **Owner's discretionary expenses:** A thorough review of the income statements for the past three years must be performed, to ensure all owner's discretionary expenses are added back. Typically the largest of the addbacks are owner expenses that one could argue are not specifically related to the operations of the business. I make no judgement here, or provide any opinion about the tax deductibility of such items—suffice it to say that, although the income statement may include expenses for a crew of five people to operate an 80-foot yacht personally owned by the company's family, these expenses can be adjusted out of reported expenses. (And yes, I actually sold a company with that exact situation, except that the yacht was not 80 feet long. That change was made to protect the innocent.) To ensure all owner's discretionary expenses are added back, a thorough review of the income statements for the past three years must be done. These adjustments should be made regardless of any feelings of embarrassment by the owner.

- **Owner's compensation:** It is not unusual for a company owner to be paid at a level well exceeding market rate. Actual compensation paid to the owner(s) should be adjusted to market-rate compensation, the rate that is assumed to be paid post-close. Once again, the goal here is make adjustments to actual expenses to provide the buyer with an estimate of the cash flow the business is projected to produce after the sale is concluded. Salary surveys can be used to determine a fair wage for this adjustment. In many cases, the buyer will use their own internal compensation levels.

    Compensation adjustments do not always increase seller's recast EBITDA. For tax purposes, sometimes owners limit their compensation and receive cash flow from distributions, which may be non-taxable, depending on tax basis. In those cases, an adjustment to market rate could result in a decrease in recast EBITDA.

    In those cases where recast EBITDA is adjusted downward because actual compensation is below a market rate level, the seller should consider offering to maintain his or her salary at the current level and work for a below market rate level, if agreed to by the buyer. Here is why: for every dollar EBITDA is reduced, the value of the business decreases by an order of magnitude of the EBITDA multiple. Do the math to determine if the "lost"

FINANCIAL DATA

wages post-close are less than the negative adjustment to value. If they are, then offer to keep wages at the current level.
- **Non-recurring items:** In addition to the owner's discretionary expenses, there may be other expenses that are non-recurring in nature and that should be excluded to give the buyer a more accurate accounting of the target companies earnings capacity. An example of such an adjustment would be legal costs incurred for a rare lawsuit. If the company can demonstrate that it does not have an ongoing record of litigation, these costs should be adjusted out of that year's income statement. Other areas to explore as non-recurring include unusual severance payments to terminated employees, atypical write-offs of inventory or accounts receivable, or legal and filing fees incurred for a once-every-ten-years intellectual property filing.

    Non-recurring item adjustments should also be applied to areas that may yield a negative recast EBITDA adjustment, including one-time revenue from a windfall contract that is not expected to recur in the next few years. Along the same lines, one-time reductions to expenses (e.g., a refund from a workers' compensation audit) should be added back to expenses, unless the seller can demonstrate that its workers' compensation expense has permanently been reduced.
- **Buyer's savings:** By far the most controversial of the addbacks, buyer's savings include those expenses that the buyer will save as a result of acquiring the seller's company. For example, let's assume that that buyer and seller each have sales offices within five miles of each other. Consolidating those offices will reduce operating expenses by $150,000, with no negative impact on revenues.

    The seller can list that as an addback. However, be prepared for some pushback by the buyer, who will attempt to disallow any addbacks for expense savings resulting from post-closing activities. Items like these are at least worth discussing with the buyer, and perhaps compromising with them on the magnitude of the addback. This potential adjustment may indeed be one of the primary reasons a buyer is interested in the transaction, but in most cases, they want this adjustment to be to their benefit, and not as an increase in the purchase price.

Think of your financial data as a report card on your past performance and as a peek into the future. What grade will the buyer give you?

> **BEST PRACTICE**
>
> Create a spreadsheet for the "trailing 12 months" ("TTM"), including recast adjustments. Update it monthly.

CHAPTER 10
TAXES

There are a number of tax issues that can affect the seller and that require advance planning to ensure the best outcome. Please note that the tax items discussed in this book are not intended as tax advice of any kind, and are not meant to be a complete discussion of all tax-related matters. You are strongly urged to seek the advice of a tax expert to review your specific situation and structure, and to make recommendations based on your particular transaction.

Let's now address some common tax matters related to the sale of a company.

- **Stock v. asset sale:** With rare exception, buyers want to purchase assets, while sellers want to sell stock. In an asset purchase, the buyer (based upon a mutually-agreed upon allocation of the purchase price) will have the opportunity to step up the basis of certain assets—e.g., fixed assets—and depreciate the new value, thus enabling the buyer to receive an income tax deduction over a relatively short period of time for that portion of the purchase price. The seller would prefer to structure the sale as a stock sale to receive capital gains tax treatment, which is taxed at a lower rate than the ordinary income tax rate the seller would have to use for an asset sale. These polar positions require careful analysis by the seller's tax experts, and negotiation by its legal and deal representatives to optimize the seller's position.

- **Indemnification by the seller:** Since the typical sale transaction is an asset sale, the buyer does not usually assume any tax liabilities. Even if the transaction is a stock sale, the buyer will require indemnification for potential tax liabilities. Therefore, most seller-related tax matters never actually affect the buyer.
- **Due Diligence:** Nevertheless, the buyer will still do its due diligence on tax matters, to gain a full understanding of tax issues and, if nothing else, to assess how compliant the seller has historically been with taxes. It would not be unreasonable for a buyer to conclude that a seller with a history of tax problems might have problems in other areas also. Remember the impact that risk has on value.
- **Representations and warranties:** The seller will be required to provide representations and warranties (discussed further in the chapter on "The Definitive Agreements") to the buyer regarding taxes. It is therefore particularly important for the seller to ensure they have complied with local, state, and federal tax codes, and to avoid any breeches in the definitive agreements.
- **Advanced tax planning:** Throughout this book, the need to prepare for an eventual sale is promoted and encouraged, as time is often needed to effect necessary changes. Regarding tax minimization, there are numerous strategies that should be considered depending on the size of the transaction, the net worth of the seller, and the type of entity being sold. Seek out the services of a top-notch estate planning attorney, CPA, or tax attorney who can examine your particular situation and explore viable ways to reduce taxes to be paid by the seller.

TAXES

As part of due diligence, the buyer will examine a number of areas related to taxes. A few of the potential issues a buyer may discover and that therefore should be addressed by the seller ahead of time include:

- **Disproportionate distributions:** S-corporations are required to make distributions to their shareholders in proportion to percentage ownership, based on the assumption that S-corporations can only have one class of stock. Failure to make proportionate distributions could result in what is known as a "blown election," which jeopardizes the corporation's S-corporation status. I am not a tax expert, but I am told this is a bad thing.

    Michael Cole, a CPA with the accounting firm HCVT, has been involved in transactions where S-corporations made disproportionate distributions. Fixing these situations can be expensive and time-consuming. The IRS does allow exceptions for such situations, but if you are unable to take advantage of those exceptions, the IRS could nullify the S-corporation election and force the corporation to backpay income taxes at a C-corporation level. In preparation for an eventual sale, it is imperative that you engage an outside CPA firm to review your annual distributions to ensure compliance with the tax code.
- **Tax return filings:** The seller will be required to represent and warrant that all local, state, and federal tax filings have been made on a timely basis. If you have any tax returns that have not been filed on a timely basis, it is important to address those matters before going to market.
- **Sales taxes:** The collection and reporting of sales tax can be very problematic for a lot of companies. Most sales tax audits yield some liability for the company, usually due to the lack of resale certificates from wholesale customers. Recently, with the South

RUN IT LIKE YOU'LL SELL IT

Dakota v. Wayfair ruling, Internet retailers have been burdened with collecting sales tax on Internet sales where the retailers have what is known as "nexus." Failure to collect and remit such sales tax can be costly and time-consuming to correct. As with other tax issues, you should consult with a tax expert—in this case one that is known as a state and local tax ("SALT") expert to ensure your company's compliance with existing tax regulations.

> **BEST PRACTICE**
>
> Meet with your outside CPA to review the various tax issues, and address any concerns immediately.

CHAPTER 11
CUSTOMERS

The buyer of your company will want to gain a complete understanding of how your company generates its revenue. It is always important to keep in mind that, although the buyer is purchasing the future of your company, the future is strongly aligned to your past and present situation. Even before entering the due diligence phase of the transaction, the buyer will pose a number of questions regarding your customers. For instance, the buyer will likely ask for a list of your top 20 customers for each of the last three years. If you provide this to the buyer, be sure to redact the actual names and use individual letters to identify them from year to year.

If you recall the earlier discussion on business valuation and risk in Chapter 3, the lower the risk, the greater the predictability of future performance, the higher the multiple, and therefore the greater the value of the business. Imagine for a moment a company that has non-linear, highly-fluctuating historical revenue from year to year. Being able to predict the future for a company like that would be extremely difficult, and would definitely have a negative impact on value. As a basis to predict future performance, buyers need to determine if your customers have any consistency in their purchases from year to year.

Another area of concern with respect to your customers is concentration. It is not unusual for a company to have one or two major customers that comprise a majority of revenues, and while the resulting revenues from these relationships may be impressive, affording the company the ability to expand and produce impressive profits, this concentration is a very real element of risk for a buyer. Nothing lasts forever, including the continued business of any one customer—the company knows it and the buyer knows it. **Customer concentration is a red flag that needs to be addressed prior to taking the company to market.** Failure to do so will concern buyers once this information is disclosed to them. It is best to deal with it before that happens to avoid the potential of cancellation or repricing of a potential transaction.

You may have heard the term "stickiness" with respect to your customers—this refers to how connected you are to your customers' operations, which makes it difficult for them to move their business to a competitor. For example, I had a client who had invested heavily in their IT resources and were able to provide their customers with sophisticated, real-time updates throughout the day. So valuable was this up-to-date analysis that clients would never just casually leave. Customer stickiness is an important attribute of revenue generation and will be rewarded by the buyer. Conversely, the absence of customer stickiness will be viewed negatively by the buyer and could affect the transaction.

The buyer will also likely quiz you on the presence of contracts with your customers. In general, the existence of these contracts is considered a benefit, in that your customers want to make sure that they have a stable and continued supply of products and/or services from your company. Not all contracts are the same, and the buyer will want to examine the agreements you have to determine, most importantly, if

CUSTOMERS

the contracts are transferable to the buyer. Other terms of the contract will also be important to the buyer, but transferability is typically the most crucial. In some cases, the potential buyer will have these documents reviewed by their legal counsel. Additionally, you may need to represent in the contract that you will assist in the orderly transfer of the contracts.

> **BEST PRACTICE**
>
> If you have a customer concentration issue, develop a plan to offset it with new customers as soon as possible.

CHAPTER 12
VENDORS

For most companies, the supply chain is a critically important aspect of how they produce or distribute the products they sell. Similar to the discussion on "Customers" in the previous chapter, a buyer will be interested in understanding your vendors, specifically how important they are to you and whether those relationships can be easily transferred.

If too few suppliers provide most of the raw materials or goods for your company, this vendor concentration can become an issue for a buyer. Relying on a limited number of suppliers is a classic example of risk; potential damage could occur if one of these suppliers goes out of business or finds another customer willing to pay a higher price. While every business has its own uniqueness and idiosyncrasies, every company should also have a diverse supply chain to avoid dependency on just a few vendors. Reliance on too few suppliers creates unnecessary risk, and it also prevents a company from ensuring they receive the best prices and terms. If your company has a limited list of suppliers, address this issue today, as viable solutions may take some time to develop.

As with the "Customers" chapter, **it will be important to determine if the relationships you have with your vendors will be transferable when you sell your company.** While discussing this with your vendors years before a potential sale would be premature, it would not be unusual to ensure that non-specific language regarding transferability be included in any supply contract you might have with a vendor. Ask yourself, "How will the buyer view my vendor contracts with assignability clauses?"

The assignability of vendor contracts does not just cover a vendors willingness to continue supplying the company after the sale closes. It extends to pricing. Will the price being paid by the seller increase for the buyer or remain the same. For the buyer, if material costs will increase post-close, then the business value must be adjusted accordingly, as future EBITDA will be lower.

Adopting the Seller's Mindset early on forces you to place your company in the best possible position to one day sell your company.

> **BEST PRACTICE**
>
> If you have vendor contracts, ensure they are transferable.

CHAPTER 13
CAPITAL EXPENDITURES

Asset-rich companies must be very strategic when preparing their companies for sale. During due diligence, buyers will analyze a detailed fixed asset listing of the company to ensure they understand the quantity, condition, use, and value of the existing fixed assets. Buyers will also want to understand what capital expenditures will be needed over the next several years.

In preparing for the sale of your business, you should maintain a current, detailed listing of all of your fixed assets. This listing should be updated every time a fixed asset is acquired or disposed of, and should be reviewed semiannually. This schedule should, of course, tie out to the general ledger. Having this schedule in an up-to-date condition will not only be a good management tool for the business, but will also save a lot of time during the due diligence phase.

As part of your regular budget and forecasting process, you should maintain a list of future capital expenditure purchases you plan to make. Comprehensive financial analysis should also be included for these items to disclose their necessity, projected benefits, and estimated paybacks. If your future plans are not firmed up yet, you can present an estimate of future capital expenditures by using a range of figures or different case scenarios.

RUN IT LIKE YOU'LL SELL IT

Once again: **the Seller's Mindset approach requires you to run your business in a manner that the buyer will recognize is based on the long-term and is supported by sound financial analysis.** If your equipment is old or in disrepair, the buyer will see through that and will lower the offering price to account for the expenditure that the buyer will have to make post-close. In addition, if you do not have enough equipment or the right equipment to do the work that you have, the buyer will also adjust the price.

On the other end of the spectrum, you should analyze your existing capital equipment to determine if you have any items that are not being utilized. Excess or unused equipment that is just sitting around should be sold off prior to going to market. Should you decide to keep this equipment going into a sale, you will likely not receive the value for it from the buyer. However, a strategic buyer may have uses for this excess equipment and is willing to factor this into the offer. Understanding the motivations of a potential buyer is critical.

The other benefit in getting rid of unneeded equipment is a more efficiently-run company that is also more visually appealing.

A clean, like-new and well-organized facility is exactly what the Seller's Mindset philosophy promotes. The first impression that a buyer has when visiting your company is particularly important—a neat office and factory floor indicates that the company is well-run and efficient. The first impression provides an important foundation for how the buyer will view your company in other areas. Adopting the Seller's Mindset mentality means you should always expect VIP visitors to pay you a visit, just like being prepared for your in-laws dropping in for a surprise visit or having an open house without any warning.

I have an easy way of getting a visual on what a guest sees when visiting your company. Make a video using your smart phone. Start in the parking lot where the visitor would park,

CAPITAL EXPENDITURES

then continue filming the video to your front entrance, into your waiting area, throughout your offices and warehouse/factory floor, into storage areas, and through other parts of your company. This includes your bathrooms, which tell a lot about your company's overall cleanliness and organization. When you are done, watch your video and take notes—you may need more than one sheet of paper.

It's possible you will have several areas to improve. Perhaps the parking lot needs repaving, the windows may need cleaning, the carpeting may need replacement, the signage may need updating, etc. Spend the necessary time to ensure your company looks as presentable as possible to a potential buyer. While some of these improvements might just be cosmetic in nature, they will still be viewed favorably by the buyer. Don't forget that the Seller's Mindset we discussed in Chapter 1 includes understanding the buyer's perspective.

In the next chapter, we will discuss the impact on your net sale proceeds of taking on debt to finance the purchase of capital assets.

> **BEST PRACTICE**
>
> Create a detailed fixed asset listing and incorporate it into how you run the business.

CHAPTER 14
DEBT

If you are similar to most business owners, debt has likely played an important role in the growth of your company. Whether to acquire new equipment, open a new location, or bring to market a new product line, you probably funded those projects by borrowing money. To approve loaning you this money, your lender likely required some degree of financial analysis on the project to ensure that the funds were being put to good use and that the funds would eventually be paid back.

In preparing your company for sale, it is important to understand how debt will be handled by a potential buyer. For a typical "cash free/debt free" asset purchase, the buyer receives all assets (except for cash) and assumes all liabilities, except for interest-bearing debt. You, as the seller, will be required to pay off all interest-bearing debt prior to or at the closing. The buyer wants to acquire your assets free and clear of any claims or encumbrances. Since most, if not all, of your interest-bearing debt is likely subject to a UCC-1 filing, that puts the lender in the first position on a lien on the assets of your business. The buyer does not want this lien to exist at the closing, as it will prevent the buyer from borrowing any funds to pay you and allow the buyer's lender to assume that first lien position.

RUN IT LIKE YOU'LL SELL IT

It is important that you manage the process of adding new capital equipment to your company close to the date you will be starting to market your business if you will need to finance this with interest-bearing debt.

If it were not for an impending sale of your business, this type of purchase would be very straightforward. You would borrow the money from the bank and acquire a piece of equipment, resulting in an increase in assets and a corresponding increase in debt. The complication occurs with how assets and liabilities are handled in an asset purchase, where the buyer will receive all of your fixed assets (unless you negotiate to keep some, e.g., your company car). But on the other side of the balance sheet, you will be responsible to pay off any interest-bearing debt. This arrangement has the potential for you to pay off debt with no offsetting benefit in the purchase price for the capital expenditures that you purchased with that debt, and the result is a dollar-for-dollar reduction in your net proceeds. Since this new equipment will become the property of the buyer, while you will be responsible for paying off the related debt, you may want to consider alternative financing methods to acquire this equipment, such as an operating lease that may be assumed by the buyer.

BEST PRACTICE

Analyze your planned capital expenditure purchases and explore various types of debt to fund them.

CHAPTER 15
OWNERSHIP

Few people enter into a relationship anticipating that something might go wrong or potentially jeopardize the survivability of the connection. Whether it is a marriage or some type of business relationship, the focus is initially on the positive, with little preparation for future disagreements. And when those disputes do surface down the road, the chance for a successful outcome can be significantly reduced by the structure of the company.

I have a client who owned half his company along with an absentee partner, who owned the other half. While the other partner never stepped foot inside the company and never did any work to contribute to the company's growth and success, the absentee partner was able to successfully prevent his partner from selling the business.

It sounds perfectly logical to start a company with two partners each owning 50% of the overall entity. Rarely does one partner have control over the entity and the actions of the other partner. But what if something does go wrong? What if one partner wants to take the company in one direction, while the other partner wants to go a different way? How are these impasses resolved?

RUN IT LIKE YOU'LL SELL IT

As in the case of my client's business, what if one partner wants to sell and the other one does not? Or, what if both partners want to sell, but cannot come to a decision on the value of the business?

These scenarios, unfortunately, do occur. And they can create real problems for the parties involved. For most companies, with two owners each owning half of the company, these types of impasses could make it virtually impossible to sell the business.

There are several things that can be done to avoid these negative scenarios. **The first solution is to have what is known as a "Buy Sell Agreement," which dictates the terms by which one partner can be bought out by the other partner, without unduly burdening the company financially. The Buy Sell Agreement will dictate how the company will be valued at the time one of the partners exits the business, along with the time frame to be used for the buyout.**

An alternative solution to avoid a potential stalemate is to appoint one of the partners as the manager, with the ability to make key decisions for the entity. The "minority" owner could be compensated or otherwise rewarded for relinquishing these rights to the other partner.

> *I recently spoke to Leib Orlanski, a partner with the international law firm of K&L Gates. (Leib and I once worked together on a sale of our client's business to a publicly-traded company.) I asked Leib to give me an example of an ownership issue that negatively affected a sale. Here's what he said: "We represented several private equity funds that were looking to acquire a dredging business that, for tax reasons, was organized as several sister companies: one that owned the dredging equipment, one that employed the workers, and one that billed the master company for its services, which in turn billed the ultimate customers. Each company had its own separate financials. When the private equity funds looked at*

OWNERSHIP

the complicated structure of the business, they threw up their hands and said, 'We do not need this, [it would cause] too much brain drain to sort this out. We have plenty of other deals that are much simpler to evaluate. We will pass on this one.'

The lesson, according to Leib: "Simplify your corporate structure as much as possible if you're preparing for an eventual sale." Remember our earlier discussions about "Telling Your Story"—for Leib's client, the story was simply too complicated for the buyer, who determined it was easier to back out of the deal and pursue alternative opportunities.

Another issue that may surface during due diligence is the condition of the company's corporate books and records. If you are like most business owners, you do not spend much time making sure that your minutes book or your stock ledger book are up-to-date. This could become an issue during due diligence, requiring time and expense for your attorney to clean up those books and records.

From a planning standpoint (and a legal one as well), it is best to make sure annually that your company's books and records are kept current, to avoid having to allocate precious resources to clean them up during the due diligence phase.

In preparation for the sale of your business, it is important to contact an experienced corporate attorney who can offer you advice about your corporate structure.

> **BEST PRACTICE**
>
> Schedule an appointment with your business attorney to review your organizational structure, documents, and minutes.

CHAPTER 16
GAP ANALYSIS

So, after working hard for decades, you decide to sell your business. The sale goes through as planned and, after taxes, fees, and other cash requirements, you realize you do not have enough money to live on. What a nightmare! Unfortunately, this happens too often, due to poor planning and the failure of the seller to work with the CPA and a financial advisor on a realistic analysis of net proceeds. In the exit planning world, we refer to this work as the "Gap Analysis."

> *I know of a business owner (not one of my clients) who sold his business with no advanced tax or investment analysis. The amount he was being offered sounded like a lot of money, and it was, compared to the modest salary he had taken each year. Surely, he would be able to live on what he was being offered. Unfortunately, he failed to take into account the various fees and expenses, as well as other seller responsibilities – such as debt – that would be taken out of the sale price. Without the advice of a proactive CPA and wealth advisor, he walked away with a fraction of what he thought he would receive. Had this seller sought the right advice, he likely would have realized that the selling price was insufficient. He failed to*

consider the Gap Analysis, and was forced to get a job after the sale to supplement his income.

In preparing for the sale of a business, it is mandatory to analyze three types of gaps that may exist for the seller. The following gaps are evaluated in the order shown:

- Wealth Gap
- Value Gap
- Income Gap

WEALTH GAP

The best way to understand the Wealth Gap is to ask, "How short am I on the investable assets I will need to live on in retirement? Most likely, there are already some income-producing assets that will partially contribute to that retirement cash flow requirement. With input from your accountant and wealth advisor, the additional dollar amount of assets that need to be generated from the sale of your business can be determined, taking into account a projected investment rate of return on invested assets and the effective tax rate for investment earnings. This additional dollar amount is referred to this as the Wealth Gap.

VALUE GAP

Since gaps are not good, we have to find a way to close them. The Wealth Gap is closed by asking yourself, "What growth in my company's value do I need to achieve, such that the selling price (after all costs) will equal the Wealth Gap?" Most business owners have the bulk of their net worth tied up in an illiquid state: their companies. To close the Wealth Gap, we assume the business will be sold and the net proceeds will be handed over to a wealth advisor to generate the cash flow needed for retirement. But will enough cash be generated?

GAP ANALYSIS

Working backwards, we determine the dollar amount the business needs to be worth so that, after transaction costs, debt payoff (if applicable), and taxes (in consultation with the CPA), the sale will yield enough cash flow to close the Wealth Gap. This "target" value is compared to the actual current value of the business. If the current value of the business is less than the required value, a Value Gap exists and has to be closed.

INCOME GAP

If a Value Gap is present, ask yourself, "How much does my company's cash flow need to grow?" Using the EBITDA multiple imputed from the most recent valuation, the EBITDA shortfall is easily determined by dividing the Value Gap by that EBITDA multiple. This will yield the Income Gap, which quantifies the dollar amount of EBITDA improvement that is needed. The term "Income Gap" is not entirely correct—in lieu of, or in addition to, improving EBITDA (i.e., income) as a means to close the Value Gap, risk can also be lowered, which will increase the EBITDA multiple and grow value. The combination of EBITDA growth and EBITDA multiple improvement will grow value even more.

As part of the planning process, it is very important that you meet with your accountant and wealth advisor to determine if you have any gaps. The sooner you can have this analysis performed, the more time you will have to make the necessary changes to eliminate any gaps.

> **BEST PRACTICE**
> Working with your M&A advisor and wealth advisor, identify and close any gaps.

CHAPTER 17
LEGAL

Unfortunately, we live in a litigious society, where individuals and companies resort to lawsuits instead of attempting to work out an amicable solution to disagreements. Some industries are more prone to lawsuits than others, finding themselves in the courtroom on a regular basis. What is your company's history with legal matters?

Regardless of the reason, or how correct you may think you are, if your company is regularly filing or answering lawsuits and expending sizable amounts of financial resources and management time in litigation matters, you are going to lose points with most buyers. And the reason is quite simple: litigation is a risky business.

Several years ago, I had a client who had what I thought was an excellent complaint against a lender. I contacted a close friend of mine, who is an outstanding attorney, and explained the matter to him. After pouring through the documents and asking quite a few questions, he made the following statement to me: "You have a slam dunk case, Wayne...and a 50/50 chance of winning." He went on to explain himself further, telling me that litigation is a risky business, and the outcome is not always based on the evidence or on fairness. In handing down a verdict, the judge might be in a bad mood, or not like the color of your tie, or may have interpreted the evidence differently than you did. In any regard, trying to predict the outcome of a lawsuit is not easy, and you may have to spend sizable amounts of money along the way.

How will a buyer react to a company that is constantly involved in litigation, whether as a plaintiff or a defendant? Typically not favorably, unless you are in an industry that just happens to find itself in the courtroom as part of its business model.

I was Vice President of Finance for a manufacturing company that sold a consumer product. We sold a lot of units at local county fairs each summer that required a very low down payment at the time of purchase. In spite of the contract clearly stating that "All Sales are Final", some customers got home, changed their mind and demanded a refund of their deposits. The Company ended up in small claims court on a regular basis, where they (or should I say "I"?) won over 85% of the cases. In cases such as this one, perhaps the buyer will take it in stride and not evaluate the high litigation activity as a negative. However, most buyers will perceive litigation as a potential red flag and will want to investigate it further.

The buyer will ask you to make a representation that there are no pending or potential lawsuits, other than those you have already disclosed. In addition, the buyer will require the seller to be responsible for all legal matters that exist at the closing date, or that occur post-close for actions of the company before the closing.

LEGAL

As part of your planning process in getting your business ready for sale, it would be a good idea to reduce your litigation activities, if that is possible for your company in your industry.

> **BEST PRACTICE**
>
> Examine your current litigation activity and consult with your legal counsel to determine if you can reduce this activity.

CHAPTER 18
EMPLOYEES

The aphorism that "people are your greatest asset" is true for most companies. Your people are the only assets that walk out of your office each night and (hopefully) return the next day. The quality of your staff is critically important in growing and improving your company over time. **A smart, well-run company is constantly finding ways to increase the quality of its personnel through proper training and mentorship, as well as seeking out the best available talent.**

A typical buyer will look at several aspects of your staffing:

- **The role of the owner:** For many companies, the owner plays a critical role in day-to-day operations and in the overall direction of the company. This situation may work well if the company is not considering a sale; however, in preparation for an eventual sale, it may be necessary to diminish the role of the owner by promoting a strong manager from within the company, or in recruiting someone from the outside.

    Remember how important risk is. For a buyer, there may be tremendous risk in having the owner running the same company that he or she just sold after receiving a sizeable amount of money. Most buyers may find it implausible to expect the seller to have the same level of dedication and hard work that was exhibited prior to the sale.

Implementing a succession plan accomplishes three benefits for the selling company.
- ○ First, the company is able to strengthen its management team by increasing its planning and decision-making resources. Think of this as deepening the bench.
- ○ Second, the owner can start to spend less time at the company and start to get a feel for life after the sale.
- ○ Third, the buyer will not be concerned with the overall management of the business that they are buying

Clients occasionally question the need to have this succession plan in place before the buyer is identified. After all, what if the buyer has management resources to assume the role of the selling owner? My quick answer: "What if they don't?" Developing and implementing a succession plan takes time, and may not be successful on the first try. In addition, even if the buyer has an executive available to run the selling company, that transition will be easier with a successor manager in place, instead of having to displace the selling owner. Less risk equals higher value.

- **The organization chart:** The buyer will want to evaluate the organization chart to determine the strength of the management team, identify any openings to be filled, and to assess if any duplicate positions exist. During this process, the seller should consider the "ideal" organization, without regard to existing employees that the company may have been carrying despite poor performance.
- **Compensation factors of your existing staff:** Even before the LOI is presented, it is not unusual for the buyer to request the personnel list, with corresponding compensation data. This information can be presented in a redacted manner, so as to

reduce the risk to the selling company. One of the reasons the buyer requests this is to determine if compensation levels are at market-rate levels, or if they will need to be adjusted post-close. For example, if the selling company is paying its workers at a level below market rate, the buyer may increase expenses and therefore lower reported and forecast earnings. Adjustments going the other way are a little more problematic—in other words, if the selling company is paying its employees at a rate higher than market level, the buyer will have to determine if it will be possible to lower those compensation levels post-close.

- **Turnover history:** Would you view two companies the same way if I told you Company A had an average employee turnover of 75% annually, while Company B's typical employee had been with the Company for 11 years? Of course not. A company with a high turnover indicates turmoil, instability, and management problems, to name a few. On the other hand, a company with a lot of long-term employees signifies a happy workplace, satisfied people, and the ability of the organization to operate at a more productive level. Most buyers will be impressed with a company that has low turnover.

- **Workers' compensation and other labor issues:** Do you know your company's workers' compensation experience modification ("ex-mod") figure? (How's that for a pick-up line at a bar?) If you do not know it, you need to know it now. It is a co-efficient that determines your workers' compensation insurance rates. The higher your ex-mod, the higher your rates.

    How is your ex-mod determined? Your employee injury history. It is a rolling three-year calculation. Everyone starts out at 1.00, meaning you pay the stated rate for workers' compensation insurance coverage. If you have no claims, your ex-mod (and therefore your rates) go down. If you have injuries, rates go up.

RUN IT LIKE YOU'LL SELL IT

Why do buyers care about your ex-mod? Because it is an indication of how safe your work environment is, or could be an indicator about the quality of your management staff.

> *Let me share with you a story about a former client whose company I sold. Bill did not have the most exciting business, but his company did have a very consistent track record of financial performance. What aspect of his business was most responsible for this? His employees. I used to love going into the lunchroom to see the "Hall of Fame" wall, where long-term employees were celebrated for their longevity with the company. Bill ran his company with respect, mentoring, and accountability. He obviously was doing something right to be able to retain employees for multiple decades. I always made sure to include the lunchroom in my tour for potential buyers.*

The buyer will also want to explore other potential personnel issues, such as your history with employee-related litigation, like sexual harassment or wrongful termination, and your company's involvement with unions.

As part of the Seller's Mindset paradigm, identify those areas in your company that will be negatively viewed by a buyer. As the owner, develop your succession plan and check your ego at the door. Examine your employees and determine what story you can tell about them. A stable workforce is less risky, and we know what that means!

BEST PRACTICE

As the owner, start to groom your successor. If you do not know who that is, begin to search today.

CHAPTER 19
REAL ESTATE

For many companies, **the real estate in which the business operates can become part of the overall negotiation for the sale of the business.** I have been involved in many transactions in which the real estate was a mandatory asset in the sale of the business. Without the real estate, the buyer was not interested in just buying the business.

A buyer will explore various aspects of the real estate occupied by the business, including the following:

- **Ownership:** Is the property owned by the company owners? If so, is it owned by a separate entity? Are the owners willing to sell the real property as part of the business sale? Has the company been paying market value rent?
- **Appropriateness:** Is the property that the company occupies located in the right location? Is the size adequate for the company's operations, and that of its growth over the next several years? Does the building have all the necessary improvements to function at peak capacity? Is the access into, out of, and around the building suitable for the needs of the business now and for the next several years?

- **Condition:** Is there any deferred maintenance related to the building? Are there any planned improvements to the building over the next several years? Has the company reserved cash for such planned improvements?
- **Rate:** Is the company currently paying a market rate of rent to the building owners? If applicable, is there any anticipated increase in common area maintenance charges?
- **Term of lease:** What is the remaining term of the lease if there is one? Is the remaining term of the lease short, and is that a good thing or a bad thing? Conversely, is the remaining term long, and is that a good thing or a bad thing?
- **Insurance:** Is the company currently holding adequate property and personal insurance on the building? Have there been any unusual insurance claims related to the property?

> **BEST PRACTICE**
>
> To understand market rate data, keep a file on real estate transactions in your area.

CHAPTER 20
FINDING YOUR BUYER

Finding the right buyer of your company is not necessarily an easy task. There are many different types of buyers, each with their own sets of goals and expectations, as well as methodologies to determine value and terms. **It is critically important to do as much research as possible on potential buyers.**

When I am retained to help prepare a company for sale, one of the first questions I ask my client is, "Who are the logical buyers for your company?" After all, I expect my client to know their industry better than I ever will. That is not to say that the actual buyer will be someone that is known to the seller at this early stage, but it is a good place to start.

Whether the buyer is a strategic or a financial buyer, it is critically important to fully understand what is motivating the buyer to potentially buy your company, how the buyer will analyze your company, where the funding will come from, what the buyer's track record is in previous transactions, how many prior deals have been cancelled after entering into due diligence, and how many prior transactions have been re-traded (downwardly adjusting the price). The more information you can obtain about the buyer, the greater chance you have of completing your transaction successfully.

Because each buyer has their own specific characteristics and differences, there are numerous things that can go wrong with your transaction from the buyer's side. Deals that are sponsored by a private equity group very often have tight timeframes associated with them, due to the goals they have to get a certain number of transactions completed within a specified period of time. In those cases, delays in the due diligence phase, for example, can cause the buyer to cancel the transaction and move on to the next deal on their list.

Strategic buyers, especially publicly-traded ones, are often influenced by quarterly reporting and other aspects of the stock market, causing a change in direction. Internal factors can also play a role in causing a buyer to back out of a transaction.

> *I was recently involved in selling my client's company to a publicly traded entity. During due diligence, the buyer received an adverse ruling on a lawsuit having absolutely nothing to do with my client or the impending transaction. But the financial impact of the ruling put the buyer in a temporary financial bind, causing them to put our transaction on hold and potentially jeopardizing the closing. The sale ultimately ended up going through, but there was a three-month delay.*

Adverse events on the part of the seller can also cause the buyer to alter or back out of the transaction.

> *I recently sold one of my client's companies to a well-known private equity group, which owned two other major companies in the same industry. During due diligence, the buyer's review of the contract with my client's largest customer revealed that the transferability might not be granted. This, as you can imagine, was a major issue for the buyer. While*

FINDING YOUR BUYER

the matter was finally resolved in a manner favorable to my client, the most important factor was that my client knew the buyer very well and was able to work together with them to ensure the contract would transfer at closing.

Learning all you can about the active buyers in your industry is a great manifestation of the Seller's Mindset principle. If you want to always be in a "ready" position to sell your busines with a Seller's Mindset, a heightened awareness of potential buyers is critical. Not only is an awareness of potential buyers critical, doing a deeper dive will prove very beneficial as you go down the road to actually make contact with these potential suitors.

I like to learn a number of key facts about the potential buyers, including how many transactions they have completed in the past 5 years, how many acquisitions they backed out of, what the circumstances were surrounding the terminations, how long their average due diligence takes, what a typical document request list looks like, and how often they have reduced the price or terms of a transaction from that in the LOI. This background information will tell you a lot about what you might expect in your sale.

> **BEST PRACTICE**
>
> Create a list of potential buyers and learn as much as you can about the finalists.

CHAPTER 21
TRUSTED ADVISORS

Henry Ford is credited with saying, "I am not the smartest, but I surround myself with competent people." In Chapter 18, we discussed the way you should staff your company, always finding ways to make your management team and other workers as strong and educated as possible. And when it is time to replace one of your employees, you will hopefully set out to identify and hire the absolute best candidate available.

Similarly, your team of trusted advisors, such as your accountant, attorney, financial advisor, valuation expert, insurance broker, and banker should be the best available professionals in your market. You should assemble an all-star team of advisors to help you make the critical decisions for your company, and you should ensure that each advisor has the right skill set and is knowledgeable about the topics on which you need advice.

Let me offer a few examples of trusted advisors:

Accountant: In my opinion, the outside accountant is the most trusted of all the advisors. First off, the accountant has the opportunity to meet with his or her client at least once a year to review what has transpired and to discuss what lies ahead. There are also ample opportunities for the client and the accountant to talk during the year. As such, the accountant is aware of most, if not all, major business decisions facing the company. In addition, the accountant is consulted on major opportunities to discuss the potential tax ramifications of these important matters. No other trusted advisor typically has that level of consistent access to the client.

The concept of the Seller's Mindset requires you to be in a continual state of preparedness to sell your business. With your accountant, it is important that at least once a year you discuss the tax implications of a sale. Talk to them about your expected timing, estimated valuation and proceeds, and potential deal structuring. Ask your accountant what information is needed from you to be able to provide the very best information to make a decision on going to market, and ask if there are things you can do in preparation for a sale that will minimize your tax consequences. Make sure your accountant is up to speed on changes in the state and federal tax codes that could affect your sale, negatively and positively.

As with any trusted advisor, you should make sure your accountant has the level of sophistication needed to ensure that the company's and the owner's best interests are being considered from a tax standpoint. Ask yourself what experience your accountant has in advising companies who want to sell? What advice will they give you to properly position your company for sale? (By having the financial statements audited, for example.) Your Value Quarterback can play a critical role in working with your accountant to make sure you get the best guidance for your sale.

Attorney: In my experience, companies typically have a business attorney who is brought in when a legal matter arises. The need for occasional legal advice is hopefully sporadic for most companies, reducing the need for a regular, sophisticated attorney. The problem occurs when the company is preparing for sale and finds themselves in need of more specific legal advice, namely in the field of mergers and acquisitions. Prior to taking the company to market, it is important to have an experienced attorney on your team to opine on various issues that could cause problems in due diligence, such as corporate structure, books and records, and the company's history with litigation.

TRUSTED ADVISORS

In addition, an attorney who specializes in mergers and acquisitions will be critically important during due diligence, and to a much larger extent during the negotiation of the definitive agreements. Trying to go into a transaction with an attorney who is not well-versed in mergers and acquisitions will likely be detrimental to the seller. See Chapter 25 for more information on the role of the attorney.

Wealth Advisor: Many business owners do not have a wealth advisor to manage their investments, because most of their wealth is illiquid and tied up in their companies. However, when the company is sold, the services of a professional wealth advisor will definitely be needed. The time to identify the right wealth advisor is well before the sale is completed, for several reasons. First, different firms have distinct approaches and individual wealth advisors have their own personalities and idiosyncrasies. Finding the right advisor that will fit your needs may take some time. In addition, the wealth advisor will need to be brought in early on in the process to help in the gap analysis. (See Chapter 16 on the "Gap Analysis.")

Overall, to ensure success when selling your company, it is critically important to assemble the right advisory team. Take time to meet with each of your trusted advisors to ensure that they are skilled and available to provide you with the objective and honest advice you will need. Do not hesitate to ask the tough questions to determine if your team is a winning one, and, if not, be prepared to make necessary changes.

BEST PRACTICE
It's almost game time!
Get your team picked and start
to meet regularly.

CHAPTER 22
SELL-SIDE QUALITY OF EARNINGS REPORT

A company's financial statements are historical by nature and are not necessarily indicative of the future performance, which is what the buyer is purchasing. To improve the predictability of post-close financial results, it is becoming increasingly common in M&A transactions to require production of a QOE report.

The QOE report can be ordered by the buyer, the seller, or both. We will discuss the buy-side QOE report in Chapter 23 on "Due Diligence" in "The Selling Phase." Now let's explore the sell-side QOE report, which is proactively produced by the seller's team before potential buyers are even approached. While it may seem like a waste of money for a seller to obtain a QOE report before a buyer is even identified, being able to present a potential buyer with the sell-side QOE report will provide the buyer with valuable reporting on the target company's operations, and will also indicate to the buyer that the seller is serious about selling. But the benefit is even greater than that—while the buy-side report focuses on financial analysis and future cash flow, the sell-side report is concerned with risk and the impact it might have on the purchase price.

The sell-side QOE report explores the various areas of risk that could derail a transaction or cause a downward adjustment in the purchase price or attendant terms. In the Chapter 3, "A Primer on Business Value," we discussed the two variables that determine business, namely cash flow and risk. Without any changes to cash flow, the impact on lowering risk causes business value to increase. Therefore, any efforts that reduce business risk will result in higher value. From a transaction viewpoint, if the seller is able to identify and mitigate areas of risk BEFORE going to market to sell the business, buyers will be willing to pay more than otherwise.

Eric Parnes, a retired partner at PricewaterhouseCoopers in New York, told me, "Having spent 40 years assisting companies achieve their objective of enhancing shareholder value, I cannot over-emphasize the importance of an organized and diligent sell-side process. When my clients were looking to raise capital or to ultimately sell their businesses, I always recommended a thorough sell-side due diligence effort. Having professionals with due diligence expertise look at your company as an experienced buyer would is some of the best advisory money my clients have spent. Identifying potential deal issues up front will ultimately lead to a more successful resolution for the seller."

> **BEST PRACTICE**
>
> Consider the need for a sell-side QOE report.

# THE SELLING PHASE

CHAPTER 23
NEGOTIATING YOUR SALE

Just like all parents think their children are the cutest kids in the world, most business owners have inflated opinions of what their companies are worth. It certainly is easy to become a bit myopic about the value of your business; you work hard and put your entire heart into your company, and therefore you think it must be worth a lot of money.

In Chapter 3, we discussed the basic mechanics of business value, which, in simple terms, is computed taking into account cash flow and risk. In my experience, the disconnect that occurs between what a seller and buyer think the company is worth is the result of differing opinions on risk. There can, of course, be disagreements on what makes up a company's cash flow or EBITDA, but most of the difference between buyer's and seller's valuation figures rests in the assessment of risk. What is most critical to realize is that valuation is an opinion, and different people will likely have different opinions about most things, including the value of a business.

In getting ready to sell your business, you may hire a professional valuation expert to provide you with a valuation or a valuation range for your business. Instead of hiring a formal valuation expert, you may be able to gather data on recent transactions in your industry to provide you with a range of EBITDA multiples to use as a rough estimate of what your company is worth. So, when you get to the point of negotiating with a potential buyer, the issue of valuation will take center stage. And, more times than not, the valuation of the buyer will be less than what you think your company is worth. Once again, remember that valuation is an opinion.

Consider a transaction I am working on as I write this book. My client received letters of intent from two different buyers. The second offer was 32% less than the first offer. Both buyers are sophisticated and acquisitive, with solid understanding of the industry, and yet, they are significantly off from each other on valuation.

In trying to move the buyer's value closer toward yours, it is important to be very probative, asking the buyer for as much information as possible on how they determined their valuation figure. Ask the buyer how many years' worth of earnings were considered in their calculation, what adjustments they allowed to earnings (such as owner's discretionary expenses and nonrecurring items), and how they computed the EBITDA multiple. The more information you can gather about the buyer's valuation figures, the greater chance you will have of being able to move up the valuation. Expect to counter the buyer's offer and related terms – it is not unusual to go through several rounds of negotiation before a deal is struck.

And yet, at the end of the day, the buyer may not be able to get the valuation high enough to meet your target figure. You might think you have to walk away from the sale or settle for this lower figure.

A common way to bridge this gap is to employ an "Earnout" component in your deal. This is an oft-used strategy to attempt to bridge the gap between the buyer's valuation and that of the seller. The earnout is a structure that will pay the seller a portion of the purchase price based upon achieving certain financial goals in the future, such as a revenue or profit target. The following chart illustrates a comparison of an all-cash offer to an offer with an earn-out. While the earn-out structure typically includes less cash upfront than the all-cash offer, the earnout component provides for the possibility of higher total proceeds.

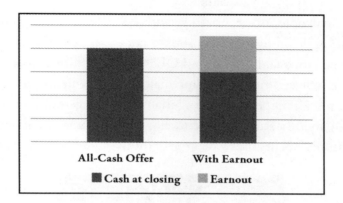

There are countless ways to structure an earnout, and we do not need to discuss those specifics here. The important point is that the earnout can be a reasonable way for a transaction to be consummated, providing the seller with the ability to get the targeted valuation and even more while requiring the buyer to pay more only if the company performs in the future. A "win-win" for both sides. (Cue the happy music, please.)

There are other key points of your sale that need to be negotiated. One area involves the amount of money that the buyer will hold in reserve, pending issues with the representations and warranties after the closing. The buyer may want you to stay on and play some role in the company for a transition period, and the terms of that engagement will need to be negotiated. Another area that will need to be discussed involves the non-competition agreement, which will prevent you from competing with the buyer for a certain period of time after the closing, and covering a certain geographical area. Later in the book, in Chapter 26, we discuss the need to negotiate a working capital target.

There can be many other points that need to be negotiated in your specific transaction. It is important that you sit down with your team to

RUN IT LIKE YOU'LL SELL IT

layout your "want list" to be presented to and negotiated with the buyer. You certainly will not get everything you are looking for, but do make sure you ask for everything you want.

One final note on negotiating your sale: absent any negative issues found during due diligence, you should not expect significant differences between the terms laid out in the LOI and the definitive agreements, and you should not attempt to ask for major enhancements to the price or related terms after the LOI is negotiated. There certainly can be valid reasons for modifications to occur; however, a comprehensive LOI will help to ensure few surprises when the definitive agreements are negotiated.

> **BEST PRACTICE**
> Make a list of your non-negotiable "wants."

CHAPTER 24
DUE DILIGENCE

Congratulations! You have a fully-executed LOI (or similar document) and are about to begin "Due Diligence." While most buyers will attempt to get the seller to provide due diligence types of items during the preliminary romance stage (before a LOI is signed), due diligence really officially starts once the LOI is signed by both sides. The LOI is typically not legally-binding and includes an exclusivity period, enabling the buyer to commence due diligence without the fear of losing the deal to another party.

Soon after the LOI is executed, the buyer will provide a due diligence checklist, typically categorized by each area of the company to be examined. A virtual data room is typically opened by the seller, who controls the population of documents and the level of access granted to the buyer and the buyer's representatives.

For a typical transaction with a sophisticated buyer, the due diligence checklist will be extensive, covering the most important areas of the company. So what could possibly go wrong?!

The burden that the due diligence process places on the selling company can be crushing, depending on how the owner chooses to handle the gathering of documents and the creation of the requested analysis. Should the owner decide to utilize internal resources to gather the information requested by the buyer, the process will likely get bogged down based on the skill set and the resources of key personnel of the seller.

The most logical internal person for the seller to involve in the due diligence process is the CFO/Controller. For the typical company, the CFO/Controller is extremely busy with day-to-day responsibilities. To then burden this individual with the additional tasks required by due diligence may be overwhelming, could result in unnecessary delay, and could cause the buyer to back out of the transaction. For many buyers, whether they be strategic or financial, they are on a time schedule to get a transaction completed. If the seller causes lengthy delays in accumulating due diligence items, the buyer may be forced to back out of the transaction and move on to the next opportunity.

How can you ease the burden of due diligence? By being prepared for it. (Sound familiar?) This is where advanced preparation—following the Seller's Mindset discipline—can really pay off. Having the Seller's Mindset assumes you are always prepared to sell, and that includes being ready for due diligence. Advanced preparation by the seller will make the due diligence process run much more smoothly, and it will minimize the burden on the seller's staff.

For my clients, as the Value Quarterback, I start to accumulate due diligence soon after my engagement begins, even though the actual sale may be years in the future. Creating an internal repository to house these documents will allow you to start due diligence immediately after the LOI is signed, saving valuable time that would otherwise be spent gathering various documents. This advanced accumulation of due diligence items also allows us to identify the absence of critical documents, such as contracts or corporate documents, giving us time to locate them well ahead of actually needing them for due diligence.

The buyer's team of advisors, including the accountants, attorneys, insurance brokers, bankers, and other specialists, will be brought in to examine your company from head to toe, looking at every aspect of your business, trying to uncover previously-undisclosed issues that could affect future cash flow. The sophisticated buyers will engage an accounting firm to produce a buy-side QOE report, in addition to the regular due diligence review.

A buyer's biggest concern is ensuring that it fully understands not just the seller's historical performance, but also the level and quality of cash flow that will be generated post-close. The QOE process is a deep dive into how the selling company generates value, analyzing the company's historical performance, potential cash flow, and operations to identify inconsistencies and irregularities. The selling company's accounting policies are examined, as are its revenue sources and expense categories, to uncover unusual, one-time issues or expenses that are much lower than normal. Perhaps a planned, but undisclosed wage rate hike, or an atypical journal entry that covers up a negative business transaction is found. The recast EBITDA computations are also reviewed to ensure that any adjustments made will not recur post-close. The sufficiency of capital expenditures, including IT, is also explored to determine if future cash flow has been overstated.

The QOE report will typically look at tax consequences of the transaction, including allocation of the purchase price for an asset purchase. The firm producing the QOE report on behalf of the buyer will do its work during the due diligence phase, keeping its analysis up-to-date up to the closing.

Many transactions terminate in the due diligence phase, as the buyer discovers issues previously undisclosed by the seller. Adopting the Seller's Mindset allows your company to identify and address those problem areas well in advance of ever meeting a potential buyer, ensuring few if any issues remain to be discovered in due diligence.

> **BEST PRACTICE**
>
> To get a jump start on the process, start to pull together your due diligence records now.

CHAPTER 25
THE DEFINITIVE AGREEMENTS

Throughout the sale process, including during due diligence, neither party is obligated to consummate the transaction, until the signing of a series of agreements known as the "Definitive Agreements." While the LOI (or term sheet) lays out the framework of the proposed transaction, nothing is usually binding, and price and terms can often change substantially when memorialized in the definitive agreements.

The center point of the definitive agreements is the Asset (or Stock) Purchase Agreement, a lengthy, detailed and (many times) hard to follow document that lays out the terms and conditions of the transaction. Depending on the buyer, the specificity of the definitive agreements can often be overwhelming to a seller, leading to uncomfortable negotiations and a potential cancellation of the transaction. No one wants to spend all the time and money leading to this point only to have to walk away with nothing.

Traditionally, the buyer drafts the definitive agreements. While that will save the seller the expense of drafting the various documents, it does put the buyer in control of the content and the tone of the various agreements. **One way to circumvent issues with the definitive agreement is to negotiate a more specific LOI, which will spell out more of the**

terms and conditions that will be incorporated into the definitive agreements. On the other hand, spending too much time drafting up a detailed LOI for a transaction that has not yet even been subjected to much due diligence could waste a lot of time and money for the buyer and the seller.

The definitive agreements are just that: definitive. Unless you have been involved in a previous transaction, or are an attorney, the definitive agreements will require the services of a business attorney with significant experience in the field of mergers and acquisitions.

This is not the time to be complacent and have your regular attorney review the definitive agreements for two reasons: one, as mentioned, the definitive agreements are complicated and require the expertise of someone who drafts and reviews these types of agreements on a regular basis. And two, it is important in the negotiation of these agreements that the buyer's counsel respects your counsel. If your attorney does not have the proper experience, the buyer's counsel can easily gain the advantage at your expense. Remember, these definitive agreements are the basis of your retirement, so it is best to ensure your needs and positions are properly promoted and negotiated.

When I am representing a company for sale, I will request from the buyer's legal counsel that we start with the definitive agreements that they used on their last transaction. This strategy provides the benefit to the seller of the most recent codes, regulations, and court cases relating to the representations and warranties that the seller will be required to sign. Bear in mind that starting with the buyers' most recent documents does not guarantee that they were negotiated well by the seller; a careful reading of all the documents will still be required.

Representation and warranties are perhaps the most significant part of the purchase agreement. A representation is a declaration to a fact,

THE DEFINITIVE AGREEMENTS

e.g., a statement by the seller that there are no active lawsuits. Such a representation is made to induce the buyer to consummate the purchase transaction. If that representation turns out to be false, the warranty acts as an indemnity to the other party. Time and dollar limits are negotiated for the representations and warranties, with dollar limits covering the total dollar exposure for the seller (known as a "cap") and the minimum total claims before the seller would have to pay the buyer (known as a "basket").

Over the past several years, representation and warranty insurance has become popular, providing third party coverage in the event there is a claim under a representation and warranty. Typically, such a policy is procured by the buyer and the premium is split 50/50 between buyer and seller. For the seller, the policy essentially removes any dollar exposure under representations and warranties, while for the buyer, the policy provides a source of funds for the warranty.

In addition to the Asset (or Stock) Purchase Agreement, the following documents and/or disclosures are usually included in the definitive agreements:

- Acquired contracts
- Assignment and assumption agreement
- Consulting/employment agreement
- License agreement
- Promissory note
- Security/pledge agreement
- Consent of landlord
- Assumption agreement
- Purchase price allocation methodology
- Sample net working capital calculation

This is just an example; other agreements may be included that are specific to your transaction.

> **BEST PRACTICE**
>
> Interview M&A attorneys to be ready when the sale process begins.

CHAPTER 26
WORKING CAPITAL

In a typical asset purchase, although the seller keeps the cash at closing, the buyer still requires the seller to leave a minimum amount of working capital at closing. (Basically, working capital is calculated as current assets minus current liabilities, which for a sale excludes cash and the current portion of any interest-bearing debt.) The theory of this arrangement is to provide the buyer at closing with an adequate level of working capital to run the business.

The buyer and the seller must come to an agreement on what is known as the "working capital target," the amount of working capital that must be present at the closing. During due diligence, the buyer will typically propose a working capital target figure based upon its analysis of historical levels of working capital, perhaps for the last 12 months. The seller is then free to propose an alternative figure based upon its own analysis. In analyzing historical working capital data, it is important to consider the impact of seasonality, as well as changes in the business such as a new, large customer that might pay invoices at a slower rate than average.

The negotiation of the actual working capital target figure can take some time and become somewhat contentious, given that if the actual working capital figure at closing is greater than the working

capital target, then the buyer would owe the seller that difference. If, on the other hand, the actual working capital at closing is less than the working capital target, then the seller would have to pay the difference to the buyer.

> *In a recent sale, the buyer—even though they were a publicly-traded entity that was acquiring companies at a rate of one per quarter—was very casual in their definition of the working capital target. Wanting to avoid the need for post-close litigation, I suggested that we modify the Purchase/Sale Agreement to be as specific as possible as to how to calculate the actual working capital at closing. I insisted on the inclusion of a schedule in the Purchase/Sale Agreement that listed the specific general ledger account numbers that were to be included in the calculation. My goal was to eliminate any misunderstanding when the working capital "true up" took place.*

Many sellers believe they can manipulate their operations to improve the cash balance at closing which goes to the seller. For example, in past transactions, I have been asked by clients, "Why don't we just accelerate the collection of accounts receivables before the closing?" While that will increase the cash that the seller can take out before the closing, a rapid collection of accounts receivable will lower working capital, potentially below the working capital target.

WORKING CAPITAL

It works the same way on the other side of the balance sheet if you slow down the payment of your accounts payable. While this will grow your cash balance, it will also increase current liabilities, which will lower actual working capital at the closing. The idea of a working capital target keeps everyone honest.

> **BEST PRACTICE**
> Perform a thorough analysis of your historical working capital.

CHAPTER 27
NEGATIVE ISSUES DURING DUE DILIGENCE

During the due diligence phase, a lot can go wrong. Not being able to locate critical documents, the discovery of information by the buyer that negatively impacts cash flow, or new regulations that will increase the cost of doing business, are just a few examples of what can cause the buyer to reconsider price, terms, or even doing the transaction at all.

All major changes to the existing business model require the buyer to rethink the future of your business. Obviously, extremely positive changes, such as the elimination of a major competitor, or the ability to expand the business into areas that had not been previously contemplated, are good things that most buyers will view favorably.

In general, negative changes in the business can be categorized into two areas: endogenous and exogenous, issues that occur from inside the business and issues that occur from outside the business. Let us discuss both of them:

Endogenous: Keeping in mind your overall goal to sell your business for the highest price and the best terms, it is imperative to be ever aware of your role to manage your business properly during the sale process. **Your focus will be to prevent negative changes inside your business—the**

ones you have control over—from occurring. These would include the loss of a key employee, the unplanned need for a large IT expenditure, or an accounting error that lowers your EBITDA. While you certainly cannot prevent every endogenous event from happening, what takes place inside your company is your responsibility, and should be effectively managed during the sale process. Much of the preparation described in this book can reduce, but not completely eliminate, your business' exposure to endogenous risk.

> *I recently assisted a client in the sale of his business to a large private equity group that already owned two other companies in the same sector. The buyer was very interested in the assignability of the contract with my client's largest customer. The buyer's valuation was predicated upon the current contract being extended an additional three years beyond the current expiration date. In spite of my client's best efforts, the customer would only grant an additional eighteen months on the existing contract. To save the sale from being terminated, my client agreed to a larger holdback, yet with no reduction in the purchase price.*

Exogenous: What happens outside of your company is typically out of your control, but can still have a significant impact on your sale transaction. Since your business is affected by exogenous factors, it is important for you to be aware of their occurrence during due diligence and to be prepared to respond to them in a positive and appropriate manner to minimize the concern of your buyer.

> *I was involved in a sale of a successful, privately-held business to a publicly-traded company when, during due diligence, a major state Supreme Court decision was handed*

NEGATIVE ISSUES DURING DUE DILIGENCE

down that had significant impact on wage and hour issues in the state. This decision had the potential to force my client to change how he engaged his labor force, significantly increasing expenses.

The buyer immediately proposed a price nearly 20% below the offer price. The deal was not dead, but it was significantly wounded; my advice to the client was that we delay the transaction until the impact of the court ruling was fully determined. In talking to legal counsel, it was evident that, even though the decision came from the state Supreme Court, there would still be opportunities for challenging the decision before it became law. My client decided to go forward at the lower price, figuring that this new court decision posed significant risk to his business and to the industry. My client also maturely evaluated the matter by determining that even the reduced price was good enough and one that he did not want to risk.

Whether endogenous or exogenous, it is important that once you find out about the occurrence of a negative matter, you must inform the buyer. Not only is that a typically-required disclosure in the definitive agreements, it is also the right thing to do. Misleading a buyer about a significant change in your business, whether endogenous or exogeneous in nature, has a truly short life and a potentially large impact on your sale.

> **BEST PRACTICE**
>
> Do all you can to eliminate the occurrence of negative issues during due diligence.

CONCLUSIONS

The journey you have been on with your company has hopefully been a rewarding one. If you have been in business for more than 10 years, you have beaten the odds of survival. You have likely encountered more than your share of adversity and challenges, yet you have also hopefully achieved a good deal of success in the life of your company with your employees, customers, and vendors. Your hard work has hopefully provided you with meaningful financial rewards and the satisfaction that accompanies that extra effort.

So now you are thinking about one day handing the keys over to someone else. Deciding to sell your business probably did not come easily; if you are similar to the typical business owner, your identity is wrapped up in your business. You are the company, and the company is you.

If you have one takeaway from this book, I hope it will be the importance of adopting the Seller's Mindset and in preparing for the sale of your business. Putting time on your side to prepare for the sale of your business affords you many benefits that you will not have if you do not plan properly. Certainly, your business is worth more and is more important than your house or a garden.

Stop thinking of the date you will sell your business as some nebulous date in the future. Pick your date today. We do not need to spend time arguing about whether or not the day will come when you are no longer the owner of your company. And with that out of the way, today must be the first day in the next chapter of your life: getting ready for the eventual sale of your business.

Engage your Value Quarterback in the next 30 days and get your process started. Put time on your side to grow cash flow and lower risk. Adopt the Seller's Mindset in making every decision, and begin crafting your story to be able to present your absolute best self to potential buyers. Everyone likes a happy ending!

But realize this: for some buyers, going through the process described in this book improves their company so much, they decide to not sell their business. Their "new" company is throwing off more cash flow than ever, and the major risks have been reduced or eliminated. In other words, they now have a better company than before, and they decide to not sell. Having a Seller's Mindset does not mean you HAVE to sell it, but if you don't, keep running it like you will one day. And always have the Seller's Mindset.

Open House is happening soon!

ABOUT WAYNE SLAVITT AND THE PRIMEMARK GROUP™

Wayne Slavitt is an expert in maximizing business value. Over the past 40 years, Wayne has been involved in a variety of entrepreneurial projects, in both principal and advisor capacities. Wayne's broad involvement on both sides of the aisle ranges from executive positions as CEO, CFO, and corporate controller to advisory roles as an investment banker, specialized business consultant, and business founder.

With extensive experience in mergers and acquisitions early in his career, Wayne formed the boutique investment banking firm of Slavitt Ellington Group (now Acuity Advisors), serving the private middle market and providing merger and acquisition, business valuation, and workout and turnaround services. In 1998, Wayne sold his interest in the firm to his partners and pursued similar opportunities in the Inland Empire of Southern California. Over the next two years, Wayne directed the sale of six companies, including privately-held companies to publicly-traded firms, as part of various industry roll-ups.

Among the many ventures Wayne has been involved with are the retail expansion of Cal Spas in the late 1980s; the formation of an e-commerce and brick-and-mortar platform for International E-Z UP, Inc., the world's largest manufacturer of instant shelters; the expansion of a successful real estate investment and management firm; the creation and eventual sale of an innovative patent portfolio; and the development, roll-out and eventual sale of Mobül: the mobility store, the most innovative retail concept in the burgeoning senior market.

The PrimeMark Group, Inc., based in Southern California, was founded by Wayne, and works with successful companies to maximize their business value in preparation for eventual sale or ownership transfer. www.primemarkgroup.com

NOTES

NOTES

NOTES

NOTES

NOTES

NOTES